Critters around the Crèche

Activities for Sensing the Seasons of Advent, Christmas, and Epiphany

PHYLLIS VOS WEZEMAN & ANNA L. LIECHTY

Dedication

To Adam Nagel ...

... whose carpentry skills fashioned the best crèche ever. A.L.L.

To Maddox Jacob Pallo ...

... my first great-grandchild, who brings joy to every celebration. P.V.W.

Thanks

To Active Learning Associates, Inc.
for permission to adapt materials from *Church Season*, Volume 1.

To Judith Harris Chase for sharing ideas for activities.

To Quin D.S. Wezeman for preparing the theme song music for publication.

ISBN 978-1-949628-27-2
Printed in the United States of America.
10 9 8 7 6 5 4 3 2 24 23 22 21

TABLE OF CONTENTS

Introduction 5

Overview 6
Themes At a Glance 7
Settings 8

Hearing the Story 11

Hearing the Story 12
Introduction 12
First Sunday of Advent • Hear Love! 15
Second Sunday of Advent • Smell Hope! 19
Third Sunday of Advent • Taste Peace! 23
Fourth Sunday of Advent • Touch Joy! 25
Christmas • See Light! 27
Epiphany • Follow Faith! 29

Celebrating the Story 31

Celebration of Christ's Birth 33
Litany for Epiphany 37

Learning the Story 39

The Church Year:
Advent, Christmas, Epiphany 41
Activities Overview 43
Activities At-a-Glance 44

Art 47

Animal Crafts Overview 48
Animal Cookies 49
Animal Masks 50
Carton Critters 51
Diorama 52
Fimo or Sculpy Miniatures 53
Finger Puppet Animals 54
Life-Sized Animals 55
Paper Bag Animals 56
Recycled Animals 57
Stand Up Shapes 58
Thumbprint Animals 59
Yet More Animals 60
Animal Patterns 61

Bulletin Boards 69

Game: Riddle Me! 73

Music 75

Sensing Christmas Carols 76
Christmas Pageant:
The Menagerie at the Manger 77
Theme Song: "Light the Advent Candles" 78
Anthem: "Sweet Little Jesus Boy" 80
Anthem: "The Friendly Beasts" 81
Hymn Stories: Introduction 82
Hymn Story: "Away in a Manger" 83
Hymn Story:
"Good Christian Friends, Rejoice!" 85
Hymn Story: "Joy to the World" 87
Hymn Story: "O, Come, All Ye Faithful" 89
Hymn Story: "Sweet Little Jesus Boy" 91
Hymn Story: "The Friendly Beasts" 93

Snacks 97
Animal-Themed Treats 98
Donkey Face No Bake Cookies 99
Puppy Chow without Peanut Butter 100
Dove-Shaped Butter Cookies 101
Cow-Shaped Cheese Slices 102
Lamb Layer Cake 103
Camel Fruit Figure 104

Living the Story 105

Family Time: Overview 106
First Sunday of Advent: Hear Love! 107
Second Sunday of Advent: Smell Hope! 108
Third Sunday of Advent: Taste Peace! 109
Fourth Sunday of Advent: Touch Joy! 110
Christmas: See Light! 111
Epiphany: Follow Faith! 112
Come to Your Senses Reflections 113
Family Advent Festival 115

Sharing the Story 117

Christmas Pageant 119
Overview 120
Themes At a Glance 121

Advent Activities 123
Sight: Seeing the Story 124
Smell: Savor the Seasons 126

Service Projects 129
Sound: Advent Offering Calendar 130
Taste: Christmas Is for the Birds: Edible Gifts for God's Creatures 132
Touch: Gifts That Touch Others 137

References 139

Companion Resources 140
About the Authors 142

Introduction

Overview

In *Critters around the Crèche* ...

a donkey guides us to hear love,
a dog leads us to smell hope,
a dove helps us to taste peace,
a cow steers us to touch joy,
a lamb shepherds us to see light,
and a camel prompts us to follow faith.

Critters around the Crèche weaves together several themes: animals that might have been present at the time of Jesus' birth, each "critter's" connection with the five senses, and words traditionally associated with the weeks of Advent, Christmas, and Epiphany. As humans, our primary way of learning from the world around us is through our eyes, ears, nose, mouth, and skin. Our senses evoke both our physical awareness of the world and our spiritual perception beyond this world. Using the gifts each animal brings to these seasonal stories emphasizes how we can better sense God's presence in our lives.

The beauty of this thematic approach is that it also benefits learners who may prefer one style of understanding over another. Some are inspired by seeing, many by hearing, and still others by their sense of touch, or taste, or smell. Using a theme that emphasizes each of those senses challenges participants to use sight, smell, sound, taste, and touch to appreciate the true gifts of Christmas: faith, hope, light, love, joy, and peace. Activities used in church, home, and school provide many ways for children—as well as youth and adults—to explore, learn, and remember as they use their senses to celebrate the birth of the Savior.

Themes At a Glance

Sunday	*Theme*	*Scripture*	*Sense*	*Animal*
First Sunday of Advent	Hear Love	Luke 2:1-5	Sound	Donkey
Second Sunday of Advent	Smell Hope	Luke 2:6-7	Smell	Dog
Third Sunday of Advent	Taste Peace	Luke 2:8-14	Taste	Dove
Fourth Sunday of Advent	Touch Joy	Luke 2:15-16	Touch	Cow
Christmas	See Light	Luke 2:17-20	Sight	Lamb
Epiphany	Follow Faith	2 Corinthians 5:7	Instinct	Camel

Settings

What?

Critters around the Crèche: Sensing the Seasons of Advent, Christmas & Epiphany offers congregations, families, and schools a unique approach to anticipating and celebrating the birth of Jesus, the Savior, and the re-birth of the Christ Child in the heart of every believer—child, youth, adult. Resources in the book are organized into five sections:

- Designs for **Hearing the Story**
- Services for **Celebrating the Story**
- Tools for **Learning the Story**
- Materials for **Living the Story**
- Suggestions for **Sharing the Story**

Where?

Critters is intended for use in four main settings. They include:

- Liturgical Services
  - Children's Church
  - Children's Liturgy of the Word
  - Children's Time
- Leader-facilitated Education Classes
  - Christian/Religious Education Programs
  - Faith Formation Groups
  - Sunday School Sessions
  - Week-day Ministries
  - Week-day Schools
- Leader-led Intergenerational Gatherings
  - Church Community Events
  - Multi-family Groups
  - Parent-Child Sessions
- Parent-led Home Sessions

How?

Liturgical Services

Critters may be used in liturgical settings that take place during a service of worship or in a program that occurs in a separate location.

During worship, incorporate the call to worship, lighting of the Advent candle, scripture passages, and suggested music into the design of the service. Share the story during the time with children as an age-appropriate homily, message, or sermon.

In a separate program such as Children's Church or Children's Liturgy of the Word, share the message by using the outline provided for each week of Advent, as well as the days of Christmas and Epiphany.

If additional activities are needed in separate programs, refer to the chart in "Learning the Story" and pick from the extensive list. A simple plan might be:

- Engage: Hearing the Story
  - Lead the service for the week.
  - Read the scripture for the day.
  - Tell the story for the session.
- Explore: Learning the Story
  - Facilitate one or more activities: construct animals, add to a bulletin board, sing songs, tell a hymn story, play the game, enjoy a snack.
- Extend: Sharing the Story
  - Send home a service project.

Refer to the Introduction of "Hearing the Story" for additional information about using *Critters* in liturgical settings.

Leader-facilitated Education Classes

During Christian/Religious Education programs and faith formation groups, on Sundays and weekdays, *Critters* may be used in churches and schools. In addition to sharing the children's messages from "Hearing the Story," enhance the lesson with art, games, music, and snacks from the "Learning the Story" section of the book. Refer to the At-a-Glance chart in that chapter for a week-by-week outline of possibilities.

A sample plan might be:

- Enter
  - Gather group: add to a bulletin board, play the game, sing a song.
- Engage: Hearing the Story
  - Share the message of the day from "Hearing the Story." Or, use the material in "Living the Story" for a shorter version of the lesson for each week.
- Explore: Learning the Story
  - Expand the lesson of the week by constructing animals to use in the congregation or at home, singing a song and telling a hymn story, or enjoying a snack.
- Extend: Sharing the Story
  - Send the participants home with a service project.

Leader-led Intergenerational Gatherings

For sessions involving individuals and groups from the congregation, several families, or even parent-child sessions, there are many choices.

If this type of gathering is held on a weekly basis, follow the suggestions for Liturgical Settings or Leader-facilitated Education Classes.

If this is a one-time session, or even a gathering on an occasional basis, offer the Family Advent Festival found in "Living the Story." In addition, the five outlines for Advent activities and seasonal service projects in "Sharing the Story" will work well with mixed ages and participants.

- Experience: Living the Story
  - Hold Advent festival
- Extend: Sharing the Story
  - Lead Advent activities or service projects.
- Explore: Learning the Story
  - Enhance with activities: sing a song or provide snacks.

Parent-led Home Sessions

Although the section "Living the Story" is designed for use by families in home settings, the learning activities in "Learning" and the projects in "Sharing" are all appropriate for use on Sundays and weekdays as ways for families to prepare for and celebrate the birth of Jesus.

- Experience: Living the Story
  - Lead family time and use follow-up suggestions.
- Explore: Learning the Story
  - Coordinate activities.
- Extend: Sharing the Story
  - Take part in service projects.

Why?

Regardless of the setting—liturgical, educational, or home...

Regardless of the messages shared and the activities used...

Regardless of the people that participate—children, youth, and adults...

...the goal of this seasonal experience is the same. *Critters* offers a fun, fresh, faithful opportunity for everyone to use the gifts of their senses to hear love, smell hope, taste peace, touch joy, see light, and follow faith during Advent preparations, Christmas celebrations, Epiphany experiences... and every day of their lives.

Hearing the Story

HEARING THE STORY

Introduction

Overview

In this section, the resources are intended to help children, as well as youth and adults, *hear* the story of Jesus' birth during the seasons of Advent, Christmas, and Epiphany. While these materials are designed for use in liturgical settings such as Children's Church, Children's Liturgy of the Word, and as children's homilies, messages, or sermons in worship services, they are adaptable for faith formation classes, family devotions, and intergenerational gatherings. Regardless of the setting, the materials in "Hearing the Story" may serve as the focus for a wide variety of seasonal experiences including: lighting Advent candles, sharing Bible stories, singing songs, reading scripture, decorating displays, and providing special holiday celebrations.

In order to use the thematic approach offered in *Critters*, the people coordinating the Advent, Christmas, and Epiphany decorating and programming must adapt the elements suggested to best fit the individual congregation's needs.

In addition to weekly liturgical helps, *Critters* includes a "Celebration of Christ's Birth," suitable for Christmas Eve or Christmas Day, and a litany based on the senses for Epiphany.

Components/Outline

For each Sunday of Advent, as well as the days of Christmas and Epiphany, the outline is the same. Information about each component, in the order they are listed in the materials for the week, is provided. They include:

Theme

In one sentence, the theme for the day or the week is summarized.

Scripture

Scripture lessons for the six weeks of Advent, Christmas, and Epiphany are taken from Old Testament and New Testament passages that connect to the themes of animals and senses. Readings for the Celebration of Christ's birth are from the Christmas story, found in Luke 2.

Lectionary passages for each week of Advent and the days of Christmas and Epiphany can be read, as appropriate.

Animal Symbols

To make the theme visible and concrete, an animal associated with the birth of the Babe of Bethlehem is added to a display each week. Animal figures for the four weeks of Advent and the days of Christmas and Epiphany include camel, cow, dog, donkey, dove, and lamb. Patterns are supplied in the "Learning the Story" section. Cut the shapes from foam core, poster board, wood, or another material. Pieces, ranging from ceramic to plastic, may also be purchased. The figures can be small enough to place near the candles of the wreath or they may be large and stand on a table or floor.

Call to Worship and Benediction

A Call to Worship for the beginning of the time with children and a Benediction for the end is provided. These fit with the theme of the week.

Advent Candles/Wreath and Words of Preparation

Various traditions abound regarding colors and displays of Advent candles and wreaths. Candles for the four Sundays of Advent are usually purple to denote the penitential nature of the season and the royalty of Christ, but some use the color blue to suggest hope and to differentiate the season from Lent. Often the candle for the third week is pink to symbolize joy. The Christ candle must be white to convey the purity of the Savior. On Epiphany, the Christ candle may be relit.

Candles may be arranged in a wreath made from a circle of evergreen with the Christ candle positioned in a separate holder in the center. Or candles could be set in a row with two candles on either side of the white Christ candle. As another alternative, arrange candlesticks of varying heights on a display table with the Christ candle being the highest.

Candles may be lit at any appropriate time in the liturgical setting. If the ritual is part of a children's message, the candles may be lit as part of the story. The previous week's candles should be lit at the beginning, or prior to the "Words of Preparation," or as each candle is reviewed in the children's story.

The Words of Preparation may be used prior to lighting each Advent candle. If the candle is lit at a time other than during the children's story, the words can be read by a different family, group, or person each week. If the candle is lit during the message an adaptation of the "words" is already included in the dialogue.

Music

Suggestions for carols are included to complement the theme for each week's lesson. The animal name or the essence of the week's focus will be found in those lyrics. In addition to singing, the music may be shared as choral numbers by adult or children's choirs or as instrumental performances.

A verse and the chorus of the theme song for the series, "Light the Advent Candles," is used each week. Sung to the tune, "Go, Tell It on the Mountain," it recaps the animal as well as the focus for the day.

Story

Six children's stories are included, one for each Sunday of Advent, one each for Christmas Eve/Day and Epiphany. The messages may be shared during programs known as Children's Church or Children's Liturgy of the Word or they may be offered during a moment for children in a service of worship as a mini, age-appropriate, homily, message, or sermon.

Each story lists the teaching tools—which always include the animal of the week—needed for the message, provides dialogue to use in an interactive format with the participants, and concludes with a prayer.

Display

Create a visual display as a focal point for liturgical settings during Advent, Christmas, and Epiphany. In addition to the candles and the wreath, an animal symbol should be added each week, making visible the theme and reinforcing the message. Considerations must be given to the dimensions of the space where the stories are told when determining size and placement of a display. As an addition, or an alternative, create a large banner and add a new animal symbol during each session.

Supplies

To create the display, to light the candles, and to share the stories, assemble the following materials:

- Advent wreath or candle holders
- Animals for display—camel, cow, dog, donkey, dove, and lamb
- Bible
- Candle lighter, matches, or tapers
- Candles in colors such as 3 purple or blue, 1 pink, and 1 white
- Garland or ornaments to enhance the display
- Greenery for wreath
- Music for selected songs
- Props for stories:
  - First Sunday: Book of legends; Donkey figure
  - Second Sunday: Box of spices; Dog figure
  - Third Sunday: Christmas bread; Dove figure
  - Fourth Sunday: Baby blanket; Cow figure; Straw
  - Christmas: Lamb figure
  - Epiphany: Camel figure

Leadership

Coordination of *Critters around the Crèche* in a liturgical setting, as well during education or at home, can be done by one staff member such as a Christian/Religious Education Director, Music Director, Pastor, or Principal. Duties may also be assigned to volunteers such as members of seasonal task forces, worship committees, and teachers. Whomever assumes responsibility must see that leadership is provided for:

- coordinating decorations
- creating displays
- lighting candles
- offering "words of preparation"
- reading scripture
- selecting music
- sharing stories.

Hear Love!

Theme

Advent calls us to experience the miracle of Christmas—to listen and hear the Good News of God's love.

Scripture

Zechariah 9:9

Rejoice greatly, O daughter Zion! Shout aloud, O daughter Jerusalem! Lo, your king comes to you; triumphant and victorious is he, humble and riding on a donkey, on a colt, the foal of a donkey.

Animal Symbol

Donkey

Call to Worship

One: The Good News of Advent is that God hears our groanings as well as our whispers and responds to our needs.

All: **In the quiet of this time, we listen for the still, small voice of God calling each of us to prepare the way for the coming Messiah.**

One: Hear love!

Lighting the First Advent Candle

Today is the First Sunday of Advent, the day we light the first Advent candle. Listen! Do you hear the sounds of Christmas—sounds of advertising jingles, shopper's frenzy, and singing trees? The commercial noise of Christmas can insulate us from the sound of the still, small voice of God. And so the Advent candle reminds us to "Hear Love!"—Jesus is coming! We, too, like the trusting donkey, can follow our Master's voice—all the way to Bethlehem.

[Light the first Advent candle.]

Music

Carols

- "O Come, All Ye Faithful"
- "O Come, O Come Emmanuel"

"Light the Advent Candles"

[Tune: "Go, Tell It on the Mountain"]

Verse One

The donkey starts our journey
to Bethlehem to hear
the news the people long for
that Christ is drawing near.

Chorus

Light the Advent candles!
Let them burn brightly far and near!
Sending out their message
that Jesus will soon be here.

Story

Teaching Tools

- Book of Legends
- Donkey figure

Dialogue

This is an exciting day, isn't it? Today is the First Sunday of Advent. That means we are getting ready for a very important day, the birth of a very special baby. Who knows what important day we're getting ready for?

[Christmas!]

And what special baby's birthday is it?

[Baby Jesus!]

Yes, on each of the four Sundays of Advent, we will share a story and light a candle to remind us to get our hearts ready for the birth of Jesus on Christmas Day.

This year our Advent stories will be about the animals that could have been with Baby Jesus and his family on that first Christmas Day. Their stories will teach us how to get ready, so that when Christmas Day finally gets here, we will be prepared to receive God's message of Christmas with all of our senses. Our first sense is the sense of hearing. Can you listen to a story?

[Hold up a book of Christmas legends.]

This is a book of Christmas legends. Do you know what a legend is?

[Wait for possible ideas before explaining.]

A legend is a story that does contain some truth, but has some made-up parts, too. This book is full of made-up stories about Christmas. Many of the Christmas legends are about animals, and they make wonderful stories to help us get ready for the birth of Jesus. That's what we do in Advent, right? In only four short weeks, Christmas will be here, and we want to be ready for Christ's birth.

Part of the challenge of the holidays is to sort out the truth from the pretend. Interestingly enough, legends—stories built on our imagination—can help us discover what is real and what is important.

One legend of Christmas is about the donkey that carried Mary to Bethlehem when Jesus was born. He was an old, gray, pitiful donkey. His owner didn't want him anymore because the donkey was blind, and not being able to see made him even more stubborn than donkeys usually were. The owner decided to get rid of him.

At this same time, Joseph had to obey an order to return to his family's home town to register for the Roman tax. He needed some way to take Mary on the long journey because she was expecting a baby, and she couldn't walk all that distance. Unfortunately, Joseph didn't have much money to buy a horse or cart. The donkey's owner laughingly offered his old, blind donkey to Joseph, who gladly accepted such a gift. Tenderly, Joseph placed his expectant wife on the little gray donkey's back.

Now, that donkey could have used its big ears to listen to all the scary noises out in the desert. He could have planted his feet and refused to move. In fact, that's what the original owner expected to happen. But instead, Joseph spoke so lovingly, so kindly and reassuringly, that the little donkey stepped out in faith to follow the sound of his new master's voice. He allowed himself to be led all the way to Bethlehem.

Isn't that a wonderful legend? Is that story in the Bible? Well, no. In fact, the Bible doesn't even say that Mary rode on a donkey. Over the years, people have used their imaginations to picture the story of the holy family traveling to Bethlehem. They must have traveled some way. It isn't unrealistic to imagine that Mary rode on a donkey, is it? That is why the donkey with its big ears is our first Advent symbol.

[Refer to or place the donkey in the Advent display.]

Although the legend of the blind donkey is based largely on imagination, the story is built on important truth. God is our loving leader. We can trust God even when we can't see what lies ahead. Like the little donkey, we must take steps of faith to follow God's voice as we find our way from the beginning of this holiday season all the way to the manger of Bethlehem. There we will find not a legend, but the reality of Jesus, our Savior.

As we light our Advent candle today, we begin our journey to Bethlehem. Let's ask God to help us be good listeners so we can hear the Good News of God's message of love.

[Light or refer to the first Advent candle.]

Prayer

Dear God,

Help us to listen and follow in faith as you lead us to Christmas.

Amen.

Benediction

Those who have ears to hear, let them hear! God speaks to hasten our steps to the manger, to quiet our hearts for Christ's birth, and to assure us that love is the language. Go so others may hear love through you.

Visuals

For the First Sunday of Advent, add the symbol of a donkey to an Advent wreath or to a worship center arrangement. As an addition, or an alternative, create a banner to highlight the animal of the week or to add the animal to a banner depicting a nativity scene.

Smell Hope!

Theme

As we draw nearer to Christmas, we can sense the fragrance of hope.

Scripture

Ephesians 5:1-2

Therefore be imitators of God, as beloved children, and live in love, as Christ loved us and gave himself up for us, a fragrant offering and sacrifice to God.

Animal Symbol

Dog

Call to Worship

One: The message of Advent lifts us above the cares of the world and invites us to experience rebirth.

All: Let the fragrance of prayer and praise fill our time of worship, surrounding us with God's sweet scent.

One: Smell hope!

Lighting the Second Advent Candle

Today is the Second Sunday of Advent, the day we light the second Advent candle. Can you smell the scents of Christmas—holiday pine, cinnamon ornaments, and hot candle wax? The sense of smell records the strongest memories in the human brain. A certain fragrance can stir deep feelings and bring back distant memories. The Advent candles remind us that during this season of preparation, we must lift our heads to catch the scent of hope. The faithful shepherd dog becomes our symbol to wait with expectancy—the fresh hay of the manger holds God's sweetest gift.

[Light the second Advent candle.]

Music

Carols

- "Away in a Manger"
- "O Little Town of Bethlehem"

"Light the Advent Candles"

[Tune: "Go, Tell It on the Mountain"]

Verse Two

The dog can sense the fragrance
of hope that's in the air
expectantly awaiting
God's Christmas joy to share.

Chorus

Light the Advent candles!
Let them burn brightly far and near!
Sending out their message
that Jesus will soon be here.

Story

Teaching Tools

- Box of Spices
- Dog figure

Dialogue

How do you like my box of spices?

[Open the box of spices for all to smell.]

Does it smell good?

[Be prepared for mixed responses.]

Does the smell remind you of anything?

[Children may say pies baking or potpourri.]

Something that smells really good can bring back lots of memories. In fact, our sense of smell makes the strongest memories of all of our five senses. An ancient Jewish tradition is the passing of the spice box at the close of the Sabbath. The fragrance was to remind believers how pleasant is the Shalom—or peace—that God gives those who take time to worship. The memory of that scent gave them something to look forward to during the work week—the coming day of rest and the sweet smell of Shalom.

Christmas is a time of wonderful fragrances, too. Do you have favorite holiday smells?

[Cookies baking, hot chocolate with peppermint sticks, Christmas trees]

What kinds of smells would have been a part of the first Christmas?

[Cold night air, fresh hay, animals in the stable, coals of a fire]

During Advent, thinking about those smells helps us prepare to experience the miracle of Christmas. We human beings need help to remember and understand God's message at Christmas time. We tend to forget or to get caught up in all of the pretend of Christmas instead of the real story. Maybe that's because our sense of smell isn't really very well developed.

Did you know that some dogs have a sense of smell that is one hundred times stronger that a human's? That is why our second symbol for Advent is the shepherd's dog. The donkey reminded us to use our ears to listen for God's voice. Today, the dog reminds us to lift our heads to catch the scent of hope.

[Refer to or place the dog in the worship center arrangement.]

The Bible tells us that when Jesus was born, there was no room for him in the inn with the people. He came to earth among the animals in the stable. The shepherds were out in the fields with the sheep. Their faithful dogs would have been with them there, too. Can't you imagine that before the angels appeared in the heavens the dog might have lifted his head to sniff the air, sensing some new fragrance? Maybe the dog's sense of smell helped lead the shepherds straight to the manger where the new baby lay.

God's gift of Jesus gave new hope to all the earth. This Christmas, if we are to find our way to Jesus, we must lift our heads and catch the scent of hope. During Advent, we must follow that scent—like the shepherd's faithful dog—all the way to the manger.

Like the voice of love, the scent of hope will always lead us to the Christ Child. Are you ready to follow the fragrance of hope?

[Light or refer to the second Advent candle.]

Prayer

Dear God, Help us to catch the scent of hope and follow in faith as you lead us to Christmas. Amen.

Benediction

We absorb the scent of our surroundings. Worship surrounds us with the fragrance of hope. Go! Take the aroma of God's blessing into all the world.

Visuals

For the Second Sunday of Advent, add the symbol of a dog to an Advent wreath or to a worship center arrangement. As an addition, or an alternative, create a banner to highlight the animal of the week or to add the animal to a banner depicting a nativity scene.

Taste Peace!

Theme

Advent helps us realize that our greatest longing is to taste God's peace.

Scripture

2 Thessalonians 3:16

Now may the Lord of peace himself give you peace at all times in all ways. The Lord be with all of you.

Animal Symbol

Dove

Call to Worship

One: Our restless pursuit of life's satisfactions leads only to dead ends and deepening hungers.

All: But the journey of Advent leads us to worship the One who can satisfy life's deepest longings.

One: Taste peace!

Lighting the Third Advent Candle

Today is the Third Sunday of Advent, the day we light the third Advent candle. Can you taste the excitement of Christmas yet? This holiday season is full of good tastes. Many are the temptations to indulge—homemade fudge, Christmas cookies, egg nog. However, we can feast and still feel empty if our lives lack God's peace. As we light this Advent candle, we are reminded to let God satisfy our deepest longing—to pray for ourselves and our world to be filled with peace.

[Light the third Advent candle.]

Music

Carols

- "Silent Night! Holy Night!"
- "Sweet Little Jesus Boy"

"Light the Advent Candles"

[Tune: "Go, Tell It on the Mountain"]

Verse Three

The dove within its mouth holds
the olive branch of peace.
And everyone who's hungry
is invited to God's feast.

Chorus

Light the Advent candles!
Let them burn brightly far and near!
Sending out their message
that Jesus will soon be here.

Story

Teaching Tools

- Bread
- Dove figure

Dialogue

Aren't the tastes of Christmas wonderful?

[Offer to share some Christmas bread with the children.]

Are you baking cookies, pies, and bread at your house yet? Or are you enjoying what other folks bake to share? The holidays are a taste-tempting time.

Wouldn't it be great to eat like a bird? Maybe you think birds don't eat very much, but actually they eat two to three times their body weight every day! Have you ever seen a fat bird? Think of all the brownies you could eat if you were a bird.

Have you ever eaten so much that you thought you would never be hungry again? But you were, weren't you? The satisfaction of food lasts only a little while. Then we find ourselves wanting something more. That's true of all the things we long for in life, whether it is food, or money, or clothing, or toys. We think "if only I could have this, I would not want anything else." But as soon as we get a taste of what we longed for, we discover another hunger.

Our third animal symbol for our Advent journey is the dove. Do any of you know what the dove is supposed to represent?

[Let them respond or guess.]

The dove is the symbol of peace. Many times in the Bible the dove brought God's message of peace—when Noah was waiting for dry land, when Solomon wrote of the loving sound of the doves' song, when Jesus was baptized and received God's blessing. The flutter of dove's wings reminds us of the wind of God's Spirit that brings us God's peace, so over the years the dove has become the symbol for peace.

[Refer to or place the dove in the Advent display.]

Peace is something we humans long for—hunger for—more than anything else. We may try to fill that desire with food or gifts or many other good things, but there is only one real source of satisfaction—the peace of the presence of God. This bread will be all gone and we'll be hungry again. This Christmas will come and go and the toys will be broken and forgotten. But if during Advent we seek to be filled with God's peace, then all the other hungers of life will find their place and we will begin to know real satisfaction.

As we light our Advent candle today, we can open our lives to let the presence of God's Spirit descend to us, like a dove might come and rest on your shoulder. Then maybe we'll understand how the shepherds felt when they heard the angels sing of "Peace on earth."

[Light or refer to the third Advent candle.]

Prayer

Dear God, Help us to hunger for the taste of peace this Christmas. Amen.

Benediction

We are the salt of the earth. We gather to savor each opportunity to be refined, purified, poured out. Now, go! Bring God's peace to a world that desperately needs preserving.

Visuals

For the Third Sunday of Advent, add the symbol of a dove to an Advent wreath or to a worship center arrangement. As an addition, or an alternative, create a banner to highlight the animal of the week or to add the animal to a banner depicting a nativity scene.

Touch Joy!

Theme

As Christmas approaches, we feel the joy of the warmth of God's presence.

Scripture

John 15:11

I have said these things to you so that my joy may be in you, and that your joy may be complete.

Animal Symbol

Cow

Call to Worship

One: Our Advent journey nears completion.

All: **We imagine ourselves as faithful pilgrims, dusty feet shuffling on the way to the stable, weary knees resting on scratchy hay, trembling hands reaching toward rough-hewn manger.**

One: Our worship begins. Touch joy!

Lighting the Fourth Advent Candle

Today is the Fourth Sunday of Advent, the day we light the fourth Advent candle. The Christmas rush is in full progress. Not all of life's textures are soft and gentle—many are like scratchy manger hay in cold stables. But there are good touches, too—hugs from friends and family, a hand holding ours that says "I love you," prayers offered for those who experience difficulty in this holiday season. As we light the fourth Advent candle, may we feel the joy of the nearness of Christ's birth—a joy that invites us to reach out and touch others in Christ's name.

[Light the fourth Advent candle.]

Music

Carols

- "Go, Tell It on the Mountain"
- "Good Christian Friends, Rejoice"

"Light the Advent Candles"

[Tune: "Go, Tell It on the Mountain"]

Verse Four

The cow provides her warmth for
the baby from above.
The hay holds baby Jesus
who touches hearts with love.

Chorus

Light the Advent candles!
Let them burn brightly far and near!
Sending out their message
that Jesus will soon be here.

Story

Teaching Tools

- Baby blanket
- Cow figure

Dialogue

Which touch do you like?

[Let everyone feel some scratchy hay and a soft baby blanket. Be prepared for mixed reactions.]

Which touches would have been a part of the Christmas story? Actually, both would be, right? Mary and Joseph could not stay at the inn, there was no room for them. So they stayed with the animals in the stable. Joseph probably filled the bin where the animals ate—called a manger—with fresh hay, so Mary could place the baby there when he was born.

[Let the participants touch the hay.]

Would the hay have been scratchy for a newborn baby? And do you think it might have been cold in the stable? Well, the hay would be scratchy, but actually, the stable could have been quite warm. Can you guess why?

[Wait while some think.]

It's because the animals crowded in the stable would help warm the air.

One Christmas legend says that the cow in the stable stood near the manger to warm the baby with her breath when Jesus was born. That makes a nice story, doesn't it? That is why the cow is our symbol for the touch of Christmas joy.

[Refer to or place the cow in the Advent display.]

The Bible says that Mary wrapped the baby in swaddling cloths, so his delicate skin did not feel the discomfort of the manger hay. So even though the world Jesus was born into was cold and scratchy—like our world often is—those around him worked together to bring warmth and tenderness. Christmas is still a time of warm and tender touches.

We must not let pushing and shoving to shop at the mall be the only touches we share this Christmas. The animal symbol of the cow reminds us to share the message of the first Christmas—a message of warmth and gentleness.

[Pick up the blanket again.]

As we light our Advent candles today, we want to remember that Jesus asks us to help make the world a better place for everyone born into it. Can you remember to share the touch of Christmas joy with someone today?

[Light or refer to the fourth Advent candle.]

Prayer

Dear God, Touch us with the joy of Christmas, so we can touch others in your name. Amen.

Benediction

In our worship, God caresses us with love and forgiveness, soothing and healing our deepest wounds. Through our lives, God offers a gentle touch to an aching world. Go! Reach out with Christ's compassion.

Visuals

For the Fourth Sunday of Advent, add the symbol of a cow to an Advent wreath or to a worship center arrangement. As an addition, or an alternative, create a banner to highlight the animal of the week or to add the animal to a banner depicting a nativity scene.

See Light!

Theme

With the birth of the Lamb of God, we see the promise of salvation fulfilled.

Scripture

John 1:29

The next day he saw Jesus coming toward him and declared, "Here is the Lamb of God who takes away the sin of the world!"

Animal Symbol

Lamb

Call to Worship

One: Celebrate Christmas! Our journey has ended, our prayers have been heard, the Messiah is born.

All: Let worship lead us to look in the manger and see for ourselves the beautiful Christ Child who radiates love to illumine each life.

One: See light!

Lighting the Fourth Advent Candle

Today is Christmas Eve/Day, the day we light the Christ candle. All during Advent we see the lights of Christmas around us, flashing, sparkling, twinkling. However, we can look at the beauty of Christmas lights and still not see their meaning. All the light in the world will not help us if we do not see Jesus as the Light of the World this Christmas. Today the glowing candles remind us that we celebrate the arrival of the Christ Child, the Lamb of God; today we see the promise of salvation fulfilled.

[Light the Christ candle.]

Music

Carols

- "The Friendly Beasts"
- "While Shepherds Watched Their Flocks"

"Light the Christmas Candle"

[Tune: "Go, Tell It on the Mountain"]

Verse Five

The sheep kneels at the manger
and bows his horns so curled
to see the lamb of God who's
the Savior of the world.

Chorus

Light the Christmas candle!
Let it burn brightly far and near!
Sending out the message
that Jesus Christ is here.

Story

Teaching Tool

- Lamb figure

Dialogue

Merry Christmas! Welcome to our crowded stable! All during Advent, as we have prepared for Christmas Day, we have been adding animals to our manger scene. What was the first animal to start us on our Advent journey?

[Let someone respond donkey.]

Yes, we told the story of the old, blind donkey who followed the loving sound of Joseph's voice all the way to Bethlehem. During Advent we listened for God's loving voice, too.

What was the second animal who helped us on our way?

[Let someone share dog.]

The faithful shepherd dog who could smell the hope of Christmas coming kept us on the track toward Christmas.

And the third animal?

[Let someone guess dove.]

The dove was our next reminder of how to prepare during Advent. If we let God's Spirit lead us, then we can taste the satisfying peace of God's presence.

Last Sunday, who joined us?

[Someone should say cow.]

Yes, the cow added the warmth of her breath to the stable in preparation for the birth of Jesus. We experienced the joy of God's touch as Christmas drew closer!

What other animals might have been in the stable near the manger when Jesus was born?

[Agree with any guesses, but wait until someone suggests a sheep or lamb.]

The lamb is our symbol for Christmas and joins our manger scene today. Can you guess why? It's because Jesus is sometimes called the "Lamb of God." You see, a lamb, pure and perfect, was once used as an offering for sin. Jesus came from God, pure and perfect, and offered himself for us, so that we might know true forgiveness. When we look in the manger, what should we see? Just a baby? No, we should see the Lamb of God, our Savior, who was born that we might have eternal life.

[Refer to or place the lamb in the worship center arrangement.]

The legend says that the old donkey was healed of his blindness as he peered in the manger that first Christmas morning. As we light the Christ candle today, let's pray that our eyes will see who Jesus really is—the Lamb of God, who takes away the sin of the world.

[Light or refer to the Christ candle.]

Prayer

Dear God, Give us eyes to see your gift of Jesus this Christmas. Amen.

Benediction

Like the clarity that comes with dawn, worship lifts the curtain so that we can see God's presence in life. Leave now, determined to live in the light of the newborn Christ.

Visuals

For Christmas Eve or Christmas Day, add the symbol of a lamb to an Advent wreath or to a worship center arrangement. As an addition, or an alternative, create a banner to highlight the animal of the week or to add the animal to a banner depicting a nativity scene.

Follow Faith!

Theme

With the light of God's presence to lead us, we can live the life of faith.

Scripture

2 Corinthians 5:7

For we walk by faith, not by sight.

Animal Symbol

Camel

Call to Worship

One: The Good News of Jesus' birth enlivens our senses and completes our Advent journey.

All: **Yet, Epiphany's message calls us to move beyond what is known and familiar, trusting only in the God we worship.**

One: Follow faith!

Re-lighting the Christmas Candle

Today is Epiphany, the day we re-light the Christ candle. Sometimes we are too ready to extinguish the lights of Christmas. The holidays are past, the gifts are put away, we feel eager to get back to regular activities. But we must not put away the message of Christmas with the tree and its trimmings. The challenge of Epiphany is to follow with faith the star of Christmas, right into the New Year.

[Light the Christ candle.]

Music

Carols

- "Joy to the World"
- "We Three Kings"

"Light the Christmas Candle"

[Tune: "Go, Tell It on the Mountain"]

Verse Six

The camel ends our journey.
We kneel at Jesus feet.
The heavenly light is shining,
God's promise is complete.

Chorus

Light the Christmas candle!
Let it burn brightly far and near!
Sending out the message
that Jesus Christ is here.

Story

Teaching Tool

- Camel figure

Dialogue

Just when we thought our stable could not hold any more animals, surprise! A camel has shown up to join the others. Do you know who rode the camels to Bethlehem?

[Listeners may easily guess the Wise Ones.]

Yes, the story of Epiphany is the story of the arrival of the special visitors from the East. Who knows how that story goes?

[Invite someone to recap the story of the wise ones and the gifts of gold, frankincense, and myrrh, prompting as necessary.]

Wow! Do you have as many questions about the Wise Ones as I do? Who were they? Where did they come from? How did they know to follow the star? How did they understand the importance of Jesus' birth? Where did they return after they left Bethlehem? What was life like for them after they went home? The Bible doesn't even tell us if they were men or women. The story seems to raise more questions than it answers. But that is okay. The message of Epiphany is the challenge of faith. We must start on the journey trusting God to lead us all the way, just as the Wise Ones did.

Faith requires us to have a sixth sense, meaning we must sometimes act on an inner knowing—a knowing that goes beyond what we can see, hear, smell, taste, or touch. Living by faith doesn't always make sense. In fact, some people think it is even laughable.

Our camel friend reminds us to follow in faith, despite what others may think or say. To many, the camel is a ridiculous looking beast—yet the Wise Ones likely traveled by camel because no other animal is so perfectly adapted to live without water, survive sand storms, or keep from sinking as it travels through the desert. Ridiculous or not, the camel is perfect desert transportation.

[Refer to or add the camel to the worship center arrangement.]

The same is true of faith as our transportation through life.

Now that Christmas is over, some people may put away the message of the Christ Child until holiday time returns. But you are wise. You will remember the camel's lesson to follow in faith for as long as it takes. God sets the journey; faith leads us on. That really makes sense!

[Light or refer to the Christ candle.]

Prayer

Dear God, Thank You for the sense of faith that teaches us to trust you always. Amen.

Benediction

Epiphany announces that our journey to Bethlehem is complete, but life's journey continues. Let the light of God's Presence lead you in each day of the New Year. Go to follow in faith.

Visuals

For Epiphany, add the symbol of a camel to a wreath or to a worship center arrangement. As an addition, or an alternative, create a banner to highlight the animal of the week or to add the animal to a banner depicting a nativity scene.

Celebrating the Story

CELEBRATING THE STORY

Celebration of Christ's Birth

Prelude

Call to Worship

One: God invites us here to celebrate the gift of new life, not only the birth of Jesus, but the re-birth of our faith.

All: **Although God's presence is beyond our comprehension, we can sense God-with-us in the sights, smells, sounds, tastes, and touches of this season.**

One: Let the reality of God's love surround us as we worship in the name of Christ, the Holy One of God.

Carol

"Angels We Have Heard on High"

Invocation

Let us pray: God of all creation, quicken our weary hearts by your Holy Spirit. Sensitize us to your presence, and give us the power to celebrate with all the host of heaven the glorious news that Christ is born! Grant us, we pray, a humble faith ready to receive his re-birth in our lives today. Amen.

Anthem

"Sweet Little Jesus Boy"

The Christmas Story Begins: "Hear Love!"

Scripture

Luke 2:1-5

In those days a decree went out from Emperor Augustus that all the world should be registered. This was the first registration and was taken while Quirinius was governor of Syria. All went to their own towns to be registered. Joseph also went from the town of Nazareth in Galilee to Judea, to the city of David called Bethlehem, because he was descended from the house and family of David. He went to be registered with Mary, to whom he was engaged and who was expecting a child.

Commentary

Can you hear the sound of Christmas love? Does it sound like money clinking in cash registers? Does it sound like battery-powered chimes repeating twenty-five different Christmas carols? Christmas can be noisy—so noisy we don't hear God's still small voice. If we want to hear the sound of Christmas love, we must choose to listen for the voice of God.

The donkey reminds us to train our ears to listen for the voice of the one we can trust. Just as the tone of Father Joseph's reassuring words quieted the little donkey as he was led to Bethlehem, so God's message in Jesus can bring us peace as we travel through life. Our ears must strain to hear—not the noise and problems around us—but the soothing sound of a loving voice. "Do not fear. Follow me. All is well."

Are you listening?

Carol

"O Come, O Come Emmanuel"

Lighting the First Advent Candle

All Is Now Ready: "Smell Hope!"

Scripture

Luke 2:6-7

While they were there, the time came for her to deliver her child. And she gave birth to her firstborn son and wrapped him in bands of cloth, and laid him in a manger, because there was no place for them in the inn.

Commentary

Don't you love the smells of Christmas—fragrant pine, spicy cinnamon, fresh-baked bread, and steaming hot chocolate? Christmas is in the air; we must lift our heads in sweet anticipation. To truly enjoy the experience of Christmas, however, we must also try to catch the scent of God's special gift—the gift of hope.

The shepherd's faithful dog reminds us to follow the scent of hope this Christmas. Can't you imagine that before the shepherds in the field heard any angel voice, the dog already knew something was in the air? And when they left for Bethlehem to search for the newborn babe, don't you think the dog led the way, letting the scent of manger hay guide each step? We, too, must lift our heads and follow the fragrance that leads us to God. The fragrance is hope—hope that rests in the manger hay.

Do you catch the scent?

Carol

"O Little Town of Bethlehem"

Lighting the Second Advent Candle

The Angel's Announcement: "Taste Peace!"

Scripture

Luke 2:8-14

In that region there were shepherds living in the fields, keeping watch over their flock by night. Then an angel of the Lord stood before them, and the glory of the Lord shone around them, and they were terrified. But the angel said to them, "Do not be afraid; for see—I am bringing you good news of great joy for all the people: to you is born this day in the city of David a Savior, who is the Messiah, the Lord. This will be a sign for you: you will find a child wrapped in bands of cloth and lying in a manger." And suddenly there was with the angel a multitude of the heavenly host, praising God and saying, 'Glory to God in the highest heaven, and on earth peace among those whom he favors!'

Commentary

What's your favorite Christmas flavor? Peppermint? Egg nog? Fruitcake? There are so many to choose from, it's easy to put on extra pounds during the holidays trying to taste them all. Although we eat so much we think we'll never be hungry again, somehow that satisfaction doesn't last. We may keep looking for a new taste sensation, but no flavor on earth ever truly satisfies us forever. You see, humans have a hunger for something more than even the greatest Christmas feast can satisfy.

The dove with the olive branch in its mouth symbolizes the Christmas gift that truly satisfies. What we humans hunger for more than anything else is peace. If we are to taste this satisfying flavor of Christmas, then we must first acknowledge our hunger so that God can send us the gift the angels sang about that first Christmas morning—peace on earth.

Are you willing to be filled with the Spirit of Peace?

Carol

"The First Noel"

Lighting the Third Advent Candle

The Stable Is Crowded: "Touch Joy!"

Scripture

Luke 2:15-16

When the angels had left them and gone into heaven, the shepherds said to one another, 'Let us go now to Bethlehem and see this thing that has taken place, which the Lord has made known to us.' So they went with haste and found Mary and Joseph, and the child lying in the manger.

Commentary

What do your fingertips like best about Christmas—the velvety bows on Christmas wreaths or the prickly pine needles? There are many touches of Christmas aren't there? The soft fur of a new teddy bear feels better than the jostling and bumping of the Christmas crowd when you do last minute shopping. There must have been many different textures to remind Joseph and Mary of the first Christmas morning: the fur of the animals crowding the stable; the cold, raw air that came in with the shepherds; the scratchy hay of the manger; and the soft cloths swaddling the sweet skin of their newborn Son.

The cow reminds us of the joyous warmth of that first Christmas morning. Legend says that the cow gave up her hay-filled manger for the Christ Child's first bed, then stood near the baby to warm him with her breath. Jesus' world may have been cold and scratchy—like ours often is—but those around him, his parents and the animals, too, worked together to bring warmth and gentleness to life.

Do you know someone who needs a touch of Christmas joy—like a hug or an I-love-you squeeze of the hand? Will you stand near to warm them?

Carol

"Away in a Manger"

Lighting the Fourth Advent Candle

The Baby Is Jesus: "See Light!"

Scripture

Luke 2:17-20

When they saw this, they made known what had been told them about this child; and all who heard it were amazed at what the shepherds told them. But Mary treasured all these words and pondered them in her heart. The shepherds returned, glorifying and praising God for all they had heard and seen, as it had been told them.

Commentary

Do you enjoy the lights of Christmas? Everywhere we look we see displays blinking green and red, trees outlined in white, or candles flickering a golden glow in windows. However, the lights of Christmas brighten our holidays only to the extent that we are able to see more clearly the true meaning of the season. Legend tells that the old, blind donkey who faithfully followed Joseph to Bethlehem was the first animal to wake on Christmas morning. As he opened his eyes, seeing light for the first time in years, he peered into the manger to discover the source. Miraculously, he could see the newborn babe.

Of course, legends are made-up stories that are based on a grain of truth. The Bible doesn't even say that Mary rode on a donkey, let alone that the donkey was miraculously healed. But the truth is that Jesus was born, and he did bring God's light to earth in a special way. It is possible that the light of that love was offered first to those friendly beasts who welcomed him on Christmas Day, for Jesus, himself, is known as the Lamb of God. The woolly lamb at the manger reminds us to open our eyes to see the light—Jesus is born, the Savior of the world.

Are you ready to behold the Lamb of God?

Carol

"Silent Night! Holy Night!"

Lighting the Christ Candle

Offering

[Receive an offering for a special cause or mission project. Place a wooden manger at the front of the sanctuary and invite worshipers to come forward to place their gifts, symbolic of offering themselves to the Christ Child.]

Anthem

"The Friendly Beasts"

The Message Continues

Scripture

John 1:1-5

In the beginning was the Word, and the Word was with God, and the Word was God. He was in the beginning with God. All things came into being through him, and without him not one thing came into being. What has come into being in him was life, and the life was the light of all people. The light shines in the darkness, and the darkness did not overcome it.

Commentary

Christ is born! The Light of the World has come. All the darkness that exists cannot extinguish that light. And now we are asked to become messengers—to take the news of God's light-come-to-earth to every place we live, and work, and visit. It isn't difficult when Jesus is re-born within us. All of our senses come alive, and the light of his love shines out through us to everyone we meet.

Christmas Day is here! We have heard the story again. Now we must become the story. We must go and tell. Are you ready to begin?

Carol

"Go, Tell It on the Mountain"

Closing Prayer

Carol

"Joy to the World"

[As the carol begins, the worship leader lights a candle from the Christ candle, and in turn lights the candles of the ushers, who then take the light to the first person in each pew. Each person, in turn, passes the light to his or her neighbor.]

Benediction

Postlude

Litany for Epiphany

One: The wise ones heard the call of God
and set out in search of love.
The voice of God is the voice of love.

**All: We hear love calling us
to follow and serve.**

One: The Magi traveled in the night air
trusting in God's promised hope.
The promise of God
brings the fragrance of hope.

**All: We catch the scent of hope
for tomorrow's challenges.**

One: The astrologers sacrificed their riches
to find fulfillment for their souls.
Only the peace of God
satisfies our hungry spirits.

All: We taste the blessings of God's peace.

One: The learned travelers
were surprised by joy.
God's touch enlivens us
for the journey of life.

**All: We welcome God's touch
and reach out in joy.**

One: The star gazers traveled
with eyes of faith.
God's guiding light
fills the darkest night.

**All: We open our eyes to God's gift of
light.**

One: All who would seek and find
the Christ child
must follow in faith
trusting God more than senses.

**All: Like the wise ones of old,
we, too, find the Christ
and carry his light into the world.**

Learning the Story

THE CHURCH YEAR

Advent, Christmas, Epiphany

Calendars help to provide the structure for all aspects of our lives, and the church is no exception. Just like the secular calendar reminds us of Valentine hearts or Thanksgiving turkeys, the church calendar invites us to explore the story of salvation as we experience the festivals of faith. The Church Year coordinates the message of seven basic seasons—Advent, Christmas, Epiphany, Lent, Easter, Pentecost, and Ordinary Time—with slight variations among the denominations. Throughout this cycle we experience the life and ministry of Jesus and the empowering of his church to carry on the work God began in creation. Those stories become part of the rhythm of our lives—anticipated, celebrated, savored, and shared by all God's people. Rather than treasured fragments of disconnected text, the Bible becomes the woven fabric of a seamless garment, with each season flowing meaningfully to the next, completing the cycle, yet leading us to begin again the wonderful journey of faithful discipleship. To understand the focus and flavor of the Church Year, the following material provides an overview of the three seasons highlighted in this book—Advent, Christmas, and Epiphany.

Advent

Advent is the season of preparation for the coming of Christ, beginning in late November or early December—four Sundays prior to Christmas Day. During Advent, the church prepares for the birth of Jesus as a babe in a manger in history and for the rebirth of Christ's presence in the hearts of faithful people. Advent is also a time to remember that we wait for Christ's promised return to the world, called the Second Coming. Scripture lessons focus on prophecy, especially Isaiah's foretelling of the Messiah's coming and John the Baptist's announcement of the need for repentance and preparation for the One who is to come.

God started preparing the world for Jesus' birth thousands of years ago. When God saw that people were not able to find their way through the darkness of sin and selfishness, God provided prophets, or messengers, to let people know that God had a plan! The prophets foretold of Jesus' coming many centuries before his birth. That way, people understood that there was hope. God had not given up on human beings, but would provide a way of salvation. Even though we live in the time after Jesus came to earth, human beings still get lost in the darkness of sin and selfishness. Advent symbolizes that we wait for the re-birth of hope, just like the prophets. We remember that God has a plan for us, too. As we prepare our minds and hearts for Jesus' re-birth, we review our need for God's salvation and open our lives to God's Messiah, the Chosen One who will show us the way through the darkness. Advent is a time to get ready on the inside so that God's love will shine through our lives and make a difference on the outside.

The color for Advent is usually purple, representing both the darkness of the world without Christ and the royal purple fit for a king. The color blue, for hope, has been employed during this season, too. If an Advent wreath is used, often purple or blue candles are lit, one each week signifying that the light of Christ is coming closer. Traditionally, the third candle is pink to suggest joy. On Christmas Sunday, and/or Christmas Eve, a white Christ Candle can be lit to announce the birth of Jesus, the Light of the World.

Christmas

Christmas is the season beginning on December 25th. Traditionally 12 days, it extends somewhat longer in some traditions. As carols are sung, the Christmas story read, and the birth of Christ celebrated, Christians rejoice that God sent us the promised Messiah in the form of a tiny baby named Jesus. Jesus is the fulfillment of a promise that God made hundreds of years earlier. God, who formed the universe and who was saddened to see creation fall, designed a plan for redemption through the birth, life, death, and resurrection of Jesus. We learn in Advent that the prophets told people to get ready because a Messiah was coming, the Chosen One of Israel who would lead God's people to find hope and peace. In the Christmas season, we have the opportunity to share again and again the joy of knowing that God faithfully kept the promise to send a Savior, and we know him to be Jesus! Jesus—God-in-flesh—came to earth to bring hope, to show us the way, and to be the Way. The challenge of Christmas is to appreciate the humanity of Jesus who was born as a baby in Bethlehem and to worship the divine Jesus who conquered death and sin for us.

Scripture passages related to the story of Jesus' birth and the events that preceded and followed it include Matthew 1 and 2, Luke 1 and 2, and John 1:1-14. Numerous Old Testament references anticipate the coming of the Messiah and many New Testament verses confirm Christ as the Savior of the world. Each reading or telling of the Christmas story invites us to recognize anew that we are the ones who need the Savior, we are the ones whom "God so loved." At Christmas we must open our hearts to the re-birth of the joy of knowing that Christ came to be our Savior.

The color for Christmas is usually white, reserved for the holiest festivals of the year.

Epiphany

Epiphany falls on January 6th, immediately after the twelve days of Christmas (although it is often observed on the closest Sunday). In some churches, Epiphany is celebrated as a season that continues until the beginning of Lent, although others observe a season of winter Ordinary Time.

Epiphany literally means appearance or revelation. Other words to describe this time in the Church Year include manifestation or showing forth. At this time, Christians celebrate the arrival of the wise ones from the East to the Christ Child in Bethlehem, signifying that God has been revealed to all the nations in Jesus. The Magi saw the star that foretold this birth and they followed its light until they found the special child God had sent. The fact that they came from far away and from different cultures was God's way of revealing that the Savior was for everyone who believes and follows, not just a chosen few.

Epiphany also celebrates that Jesus didn't stay a small child, but grew to be a man who had a mission to fulfill for God. At Jesus' baptism, God revealed that Jesus was the Son of God. Epiphany reminds us that Jesus was born to save the world. The season of Epiphany is a time of celebrating new revelations of God's presence among us.

For the Festival of Epiphany the appropriate color is white, although gold is sometimes used as the color of the star and the gift brought to the Christ Child. Those churches that designate part of this season as Ordinary Time often use green as the interim color prior to Lent.

Activities Overview

Art projects, bulletin boards, group games, seasonal songs, hymn stories, tasty treats—all are offered in "Learning the Story" as ways to enhance the use of *Critters around the Crèche*. While these activities are primarily intended for use in leader-facilitated education classes, they may also be incorporated into liturgical settings, intergenerational gatherings, and home sessions. Suggestions for using these learning activities in each setting is provided in the introduction of the book.

An at-a-glance chart outlines options. While the chart is a guide, the suggestions should be adapted to fit the user's needs.

A simple plan for a leader-facilitated education class could be:

- Enter
  - Gather by singing a song, adding to a bulletin board, and playing a game.
- Engage
  - Share the seasonal message of the week found in "Hearing the Story"—which is the longer version—or "Living the Story"—the condensed outline.
- Explore
  - Facilitate animal-themed crafts, learn music, tell a hymn story, and share a snack.
- Extend
  - Suggest a service project, from "Sharing the Story," to do during the week.

Activities At-a-Glance

Sunday	Art	Bulletin Board	Game	Music	Snack	Service
First Sunday of Advent: Hear Love: Donkey	Life-sized animals: Church display	Sound: Music notes	Riddle Me! Hear	▲ Anthems : ▲ "Sweet Little Jesus Boy" ▲ "The Friendly Beasts" ▲ Theme Song—"Light the Advent Candles" ▲ Hymn Story: "O Come, All Ye Faithful" ▲ Suggestions: Sound	Donkey Face No-Bake Cookies	Sound: Advent Offering Calendar
Second Sunday of Advent: Smell Hope: Dog	Fimo or Sculpy miniatures: Home	Smell: Graffiti wall	Riddle Me! Smell	▲ Anthems: ▲ "Sweet Little Jesus Boy" ▲ "The Friendly Beasts" ▲ Theme Song: "Light the Advent Candles" ▲ Hymn Story: "Away in a Manger" ▲ Suggestions: Smell	Puppy Chow without Peanut Butter	Smell: Savor the Seasons
Third Sunday of Advent: Taste Peace: Dove	Finger puppet animals & Paper bag animals: Children's Center	Taste: Recipes	Riddle Me! Taste	▲ Anthems: ▲ "Sweet Little Jesus Boy" ▲ "The Friendly Beasts" ▲ Theme Song: "Light the Advent Candles" ▲ Hymn Story: "Sweet Little Jesus Boy" ▲ Suggestions: Taste	Dove-Shaped Butter Cookies	Taste: Christmas Is for the Birds

Sunday	*Art*	*Bulletin Board*	*Game*	*Music*	*Snack*	*Service*
Fourth Sunday of Advent: Touch Joy: Cow	Thumbprint animals: Gifts	Touch: Textures	Riddle Me! Touch	► Anthems : ► "Sweet Little Jesus Boy" ► "The Friendly Beasts" ► Theme Song—"Light the Advent Candles" ► Hymn Story: "Good Christian Friends, Rejoice" ► Suggestions: Touch	Cow-Shaped Cheese Slices	Touch: Gifts That Touch Others
Christmas: See Light: Lamb	Recycled Animals Christmas packaging/ wrapping	Sight: Christmas cards/ pictures	Riddle Me! See	► Anthems: ► "Sweet Little Jesus Boy" ► "The Friendly Beasts" ► Theme Song: "Light the Christmas Candle" ► Hymn Story: "The Friendly Beasts" ► Suggestions: Sight	Lamb Layer Cake	Sight: Seeing the Story
Epihany: Follow Faith: Camel	Diorama: Keepsake	-	-	► Theme Song: "Light the Christmas Candle" ► Hymn Story: "Joy to the World"	Camel Fruit Figures	-

Art

Animal Crafts Overview

Birds, camels, doves. Cows, donkeys, mice. Goats, horses, sheep. For many children, as well as youth and adults, a favorite part of the Christmas story is imagining the animals that might have been around the manger when Baby Jesus was born. In *Critters around the Crèche*, the focus is on a different animal each week that may have been in the stable during the birth of the Savior. In addition to associating one of the senses with each animal, the scenarios also highlight the themes of faith, hope, joy, light, love, and peace.

Since animals are a focal point of the stories in *Critters*, and are added to crèche scenes and visual displays each week, use different art techniques as well as various materials to create the figures used to enhance or recount the tales. The following methods can be used to construct any type of animal, not just the one that might be featured in the instructions. These projects are easily adapted to different ages as well as to classroom and home settings.

In addition to use in educational settings, try one of the animal projects each week during Children's Church, Children's Liturgy of the Word, after Children's Time, or in preparation for the pageant, *The Menagerie at the Manger*. A suggested plan is:

- First Week of Advent—Life-sized animals for a display at church
- Second Week of Advent—Fimo or Sculpy animals for a crèche at home
- Third Week of Advent—Finger puppet and/or paper bag animals to give to a children's center
- Fourth Week of Advent—Fingerprint animals on bookmarks and cards to give as gifts
- Christmas—Recycled animals constructed from Christmas packaging and wrapping
- Epiphany—Diorama to save as a keepsake.

In addition to the instructions, patterns for the six featured animals are provided on the resource sheets. There is also a reproducible illustration of all of the "critters around the crèche" for use as a graphic for bulletins, correspondence, and programs as well as posts on social media and websites.

Animal Cookies

Materials

- Baking and mixing equipment
- Candy for trims
- Clean up supplies for equipment and for hands
- Cookie cutters, animal shapes
- Icing in tubes
- Ingredients for cookie recipe
- Oven
- Recipe for cut-out cookies
- Rolling pin
- Scissors
- Waxed paper

Method

Before beginning the animal cookie project, sanitize the work surface and thoroughly wash hands.

Follow directions in a favorite cutout cookie recipe for ingredients, measurements, and method. Once the dough is prepared, roll it on waxed paper to the desired thickness. Use the cookie cutters to create the animal shapes.

Bake the cookies according to directions and allow to cool. Place the cookies on a plate or a rack for easy handling. Snip the tips off of the frosting tubes. Add details to the cookies with decorator icing and candy trims.

Although animal cookie cutters will be found where baking supplies are sold, they can also be created by bending a metal ring into the desired shape. Place the ring over a simple outline and bend it to form the animal. This is an adult task since the edges may be sharp!

As an alternative, try making animals, figures, and a stable from a gingerbread cookie recipe.

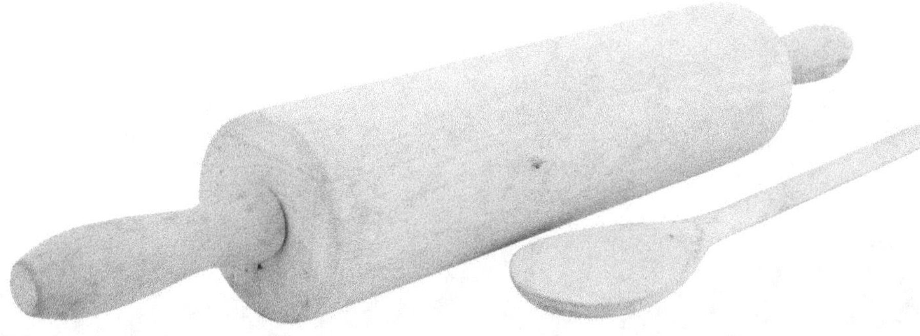

Animal Masks

Materials

- Brushes for paint
- Glue
- Markers
- Paint
- Paint paddles or stir sticks
- Paper, colored scraps
- Paper plates—white, tan, brown and other animal-toned colors
- Pencils or pens
- Pictures of animals for reference
- Scissors
- Tape
- Yarn

Method

Find pictures of the animals that are to be made as masks.

Assemble brown, tan, or white paper plates or paint plain plates whatever color will look best for the face of each animal. Using markers, pencils, and pens, draw the face on the plate and add any distinguishing features. Cut two eye holes large enough to see through and exaggerate the eyes by outlining the openings.

Check to see what type of ears the animals will need. Draw or trace them on matching paper, then cut out the shapes and attach them to the head. Enhance the faces by adding three dimensional features such as noses, whiskers, and fringed eyelashes.

Attach yarn ties to the sides of the finished plates so they can be worn as masks. Another option is to tape a strip of cardboard or a stick, such as a paint paddle or stirrer, to the center of the back of the plate. To use the mask, place it in front of the face holding the stick as a handle.

Carton Critters

Materials

- Cartons, various sizes from cardboard juice or milk containers
- Glue
- Markers
- Paper, construction
- Patterns or pictures of animals
- Scissors
- Stapler
- Staples
- Tape

Method

Turn cardboard cartons, from juice and milk, of all sizes into animals. Select a variety of containers and wash them thoroughly. Allow time for them to dry. Then glue, staple, or tape the tops shut.

Decide which animals to make and find a pattern or a picture of each of them, if necessary. Cover the carton with construction paper, the same color as the animal's body. Cut ears and attach them to each side of the top of the carton. Cut or draw facial features, as well as anything that makes the animal distinct, such as spots and stripes, and add them to the carton, too.

Create a variety of critters, using pint cartons for animals like rabbits, quart containers for shapes like giraffes, and gallon boxes for large creatures such as elephants.

Diorama

Materials

- Acrylic sealer or clear nail polish (optional)
- Animals such as animal crackers or plastic and stuffed toys
- Boxes, cartons, or crates of suitable size
- Brushes for paint
- Figures for crèche
- Manger
- Markers
- Paint
- Paper
- Scissors
- Straw

Method

Decide which type and size of animal will be used in the diorama, then choose a box of the proper scale.

Create a miniature scene with animal crackers and a small box. Coat the cookies with acrylic sealer or clear nail polish to prevent them from crumbling.

Small plastic animals will fit into a shoe box or rectangular tissue box. Cut the tissue box opening a little larger for more display space.

Choose stuffed animals of similar proportions to fit into a large box or wooden crate. Ask each participant to bring an appropriate toy for the diorama. Turn the box on its side. Design a setting by assembling a collage or drawing scenery to fit in the background of the box. Paint the exterior to look like stone or wood. If a wooden crate is used, allow the natural wood to show. Arrange straw pieces on the floor of the diorama and add the crèche figures to complete the scene.

Fimo or Sculpy Miniatures

Materials

- Brushes
- Carving tools
- Clean up supplies
- Covering for table
- Fimo or Sculpy from an art or craft store
- Oven
- Paints, acrylic
- Plates, small paper or plastic lids
- Sand paper
- Water

Method

Fimo and Sculpy are two of the brand names for a type of modeling compound which can be used in many ways. It may be molded and shaped as clay or play dough. When it is baked in the oven, it can be carved and sanded. Follow the directions provided with the product. Experiment before beginning this project with a group.

The compounds come in a wide range of colors; however, the plain white material is easy to decorate with any type of paint. Acrylic paints and glazes work well. Put tiny amounts of paint onto small plates or plastic lids. These palettes provide easy access to a variety of colors. They can be rinsed and reused or discarded.

Model or carve tiny animals for jewelry or a miniature scene. Young children or groups with limited time or equipment may form larger figures from traditional modeling materials such as natural clay, Plasticine, and commercially made or homemade play dough.

Finger Puppet Animals

Materials

- Felt
- Gloves (optional)
- Glue, tacky
- Glue gun with glue sticks (optional)
- Markers, fine tip
- Paper, construction
- Pencils
- Sewing supplies such as needles and thread (optional)
- Scissors
- Trims like cotton, pompons, and wiggle eyes
- Velcro circles (optional)

Method

Finger puppet animals are easy and fun to make. Fit a two-inch by three-inch strip of construction paper or felt around a finger, overlapping the ends. Mark with pencil to show where the edges overlap. Glue along that line.

When the tube is dry, place it with the seam side down. Use felt, paper, pompons, and trims to fashion the animal heads. Experiment with different sizes and arrangements of scraps and pompons to represent individual characteristics of the animals. For example, cotton or tiny white pompons will make sheep look "fleecy." Add ears, horns, or noses cut from scraps and draw face details with a fine line marker. Glue on wiggle eyes to finish.

Fasten the head to the tube. Make certain to have all of the parts securely glued. Older crafters may attach the pieces by sewing them on or by using a hot glue gun.

A simple variation of the finger puppet is to assemble the heads as explained above, but attach them to the fingers of a glove instead of tubes. Glue or sew Velcro circles to the back of the finished heads and to the finger tips of the glove. Animals can be removed easily to make room for other characters.

Life-Sized Animals

Materials

- Brushes, large or sponges
- Cardboard, foam board, or plywood
- Copy machine
- Cutting tools or scissors
- Glue
- Markers
- Materials for texture such as fabric, feathers, polyfil, or rope
- Paints, acrylic
- Paper, large sheets
- Patterns for animals
- Pencils
- Transparencies (optional)

Method

Create life-size or "larger than life" creatures from extra wide rolls of paper or large pieces of cardboard, foam board, or plywood.

Photocopy simple animal outlines on paper or on transparencies. In order to enlarge them fasten the background material to a wall and project the pattern to achieve the desired size. Trace the outline with pencil or marker.

Cut out the animals and place them on the floor or on a table to paint. Acrylic paint is suitable for almost any surface. If the animals will be part of an outdoor scene, use weather resistant paints and varnishes. Apply the paint with large brushes or sponges.

Animals may be used as a silhouette or may be given more elaborate treatment. For realistic textures, add polyfil and other enhancements. Draw or attach other details.

Fasten paper animals to stage curtains or walls. To make animals free-standing, design some type of prop to support heavier materials.

Paper Bag Animals

Materials

- Bags, paper grocery or lunch size
- Brushes
- Glue
- Newspaper
- Paint
- Paper, construction
- Pictures of animals
- Pipe cleaners
- Scissors
- Tape
- Trims
- Tubes, paper
- Yarn

Method

Begin the paper bag project by looking at animal pictures to become familiar with some of their special features. If the animal will be constructed from lunch bags, choose a color that matches the animal's coat. Construct a larger animal from brown paper grocery bags. White bakery bags work for the white animals. Bags can also be painted.

For small animals, stuff two lunch bags with crumpled newspaper. The bag for the body should be stuffed almost to the top and the bag for the head is to be packed half full. Wrap yarn around the half filled bag and tie tightly. Work the tied end of the "head" bag into the stuffing of the other bag. Wrap and tie yarn around the open end of the "body" bag to secure the head and to form the neck. Prepare the larger bags in the same way. A lunch bag or medium-sized bag should be used for the head.

For four-legged animals, prepare paper tubes by making one-half inch slits around the top of each tube. Bend the slit areas to form tabs for attaching the legs. Place the body in a horizontal position and tape or glue the tubes in place. In some cases the animal might be in an upright position. Experiment with proportion and placement before permanently attaching the legs.

For birds, design wings and tails from flattened bags or scrap paper. Make feet from large-size pipe cleaners and create a perching bird by gluing the body directly to the feet.

Paint markings and features. Add tails, manes, horns, ears, and tail feathers fashioned from paper scraps and other trims.

Recycled Animals

Materials

- Brushes, various sizes for paint
- Cast-offs or recyclables of all kinds:
  - boxes from cereal, oats, salt, shoes
  - cans from potato chips
  - cartons from eggs
  - containers from ice cream and margarine cups
  - materials from packing products
  - rolls from paper towels and toilet paper
- Glue or glue gun with glue sticks
- Paint—acrylic, gesso, and latex
- Paper, construction
- Scissors
- Tape, duct and masking
- Trims

Method

Create large or small animals from a variety of supplies rescued from the recycling bin or the trash can. Boxes and cylinders can be used for the bodies of most creatures. Assemble cast-offs to resemble an animal. Fasten all the added parts securely with glue or tape.

Cover the entire construction with one coat of gesso or flat latex paint. This will guarantee a uniform surface for whatever materials were used to make the animal—metal, paper, or plastic. Allow the gesso to dry thoroughly then use any kind of paint to cover the exterior. Add special features and details with additional paint as well as paper scraps and trims.

Stand Up Shapes

Materials

- Food coloring or tempera paint (optional)
- Glue, colored
- Markers, permanent
- Patterns or pictures of animals
- Pencils
- Scissors
- Trays from fruit, meat, and vegetables

Method

Simple animal shapes cut from cardboard or Styrofoam fruit, meat, and vegetable trays make great stand-up animals. Look at pictures and draw freehand or use patterns and trace the head and body of an animal onto a tray. Cut out the shape. For legs, draw a circle on a tray, proportionate to the size of the creature. Cut out the circle and then cut it in half. Cut one-fourth inch notches in the middle of the legs and at appropriate places on the animal. Make the notches one-fourth inch wide.

Add features to the animal with colored glue which may be purchased or made by adding food coloring or tempera paint to white glue. In addition to or instead of using colored glue, decorate the animal with permanent markers.

Fit the notched pieces together and stand up the animal. Make as many animals as needed to tell the story.

Thumbprint Animals

Materials

- Clean up supplies
- Ink pad or tempera paint and sponges
- Markers, fine tip
- Paper

Method

Creative animals can be made from thumbprints. Fold or cut paper to make bookmarks, cards or notes, small pictures, or tags.

Press thumb onto the ink pad, then make a print on the paper. If tempera paint is used, pour a small amount on a dry sponge and use as an ink pad. Make single prints or arrange into groups or borders.

Add distinguishing characteristics to help identify each animal. Use fine line markers for details and background.

Yet More Animals

Check bookstores, craft shops, internet sources, and libraries for additional directions on how to make animal crafts from various materials and many more techniques. Choose projects which are age appropriate. Consider time and space limitations as well.

Enlist the help of volunteers who are willing to teach particular skills, such as origami, or contact local artists who can demonstrate unique methods to construct animals.

Do not overlook the simplest art activities including drawing freehand, painting shapes, tracing coloring book pages, and cutting animal pictures from magazines.

Animal Patterns

First Sunday of Advent

Hear Love!

Donkey

Second Sunday of Advent

Smell Hope!

Dog

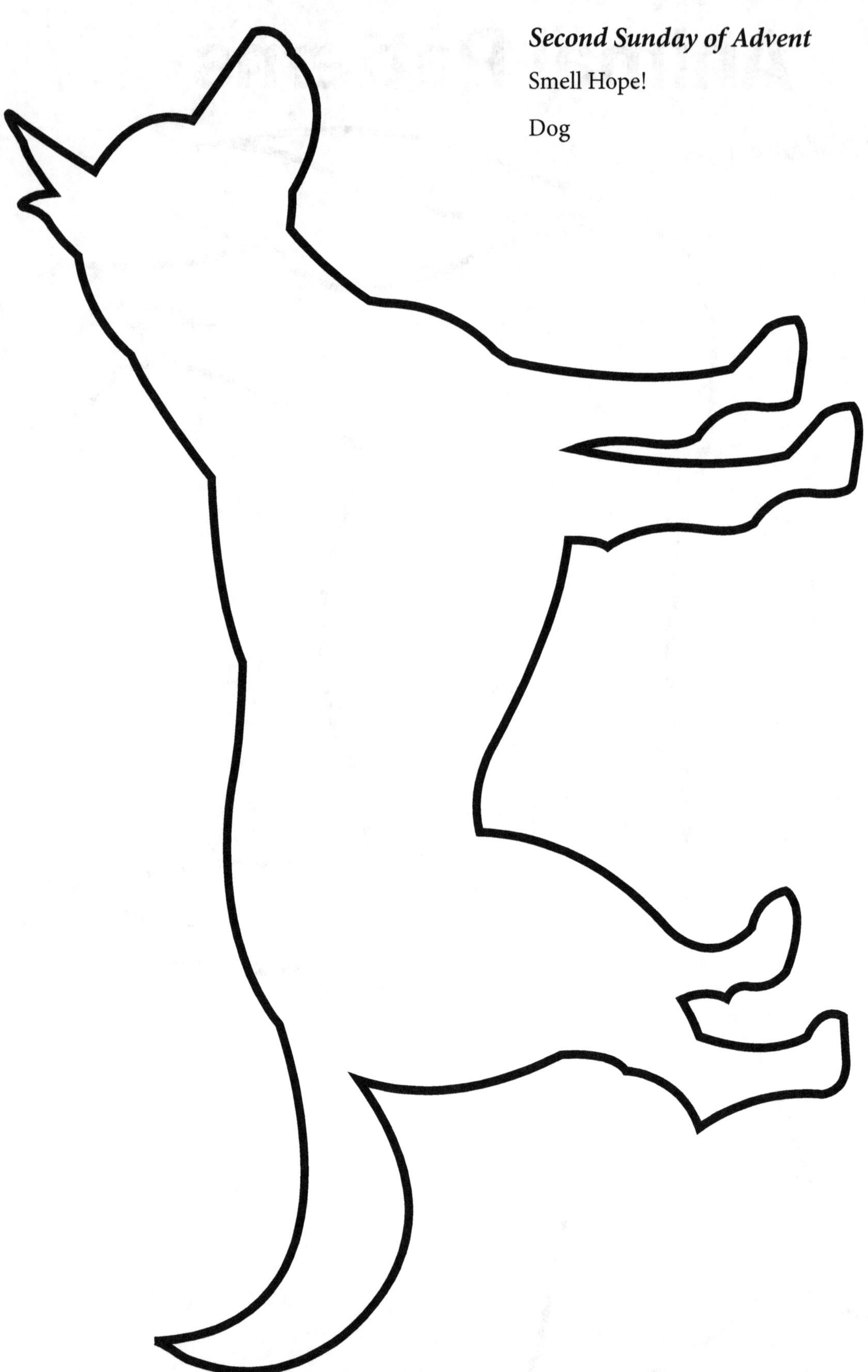

Third Sunday of Advent

Taste Peace!

Dove

Fourth Sunday of Advent

Touch Joy!

Cow

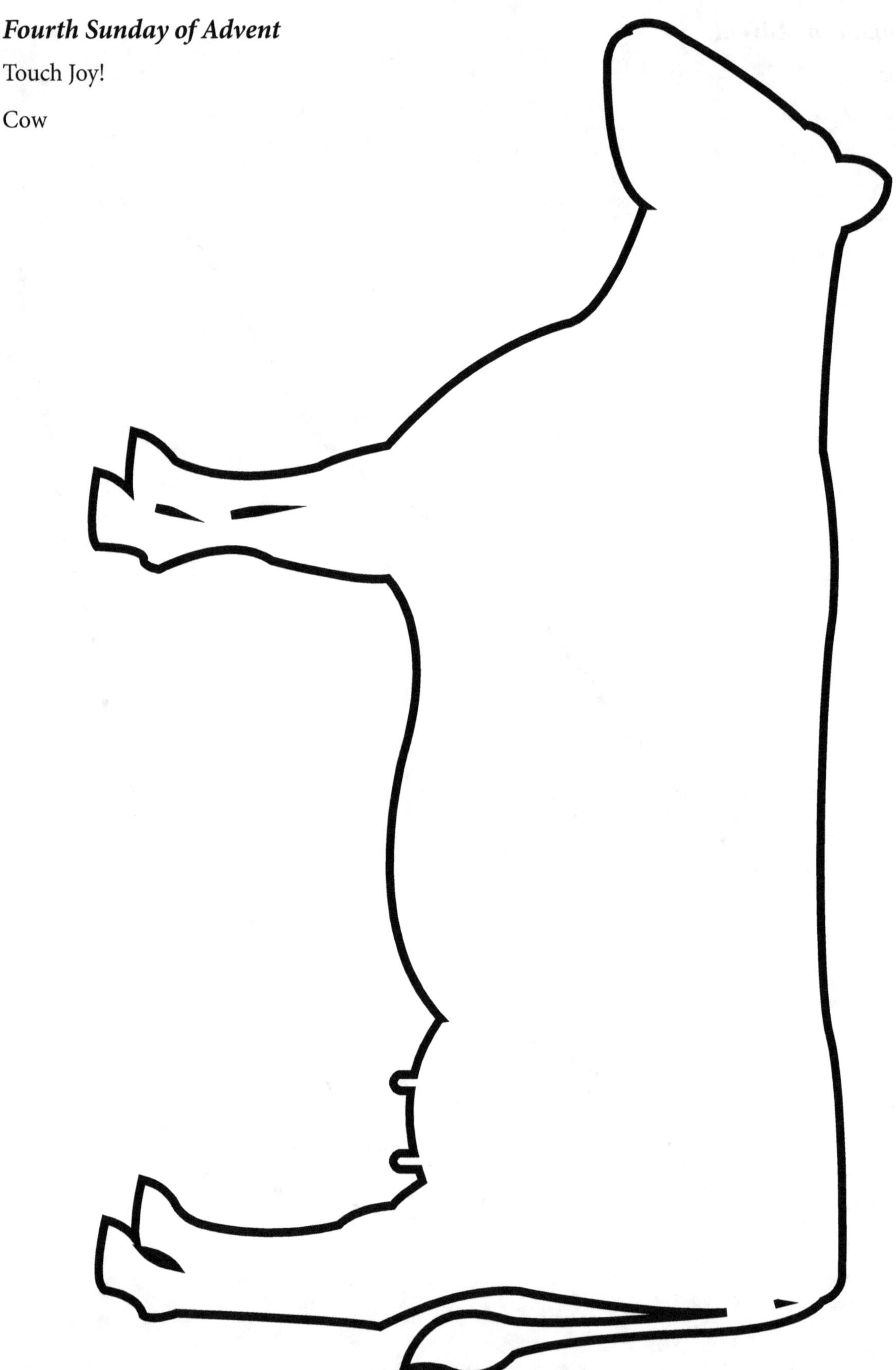

Christmas

See Light!

Lamb

Epiphany

Follow Faith!

Camel

Manger

Bulletin Boards

Displays to Sense the Seasons

Bulletin boards and display cases provide an excellent way to reinforce a seasonal theme and to decorate wall space. Displays can be simple with handmade or purchased components. Try cooperative or interactive arrangements which allow for many designers to contribute.

Simplify the preparation of bulletin board backgrounds by using large rolls of paper such as wallpaper, gift wrap, or butcher paper. Cover framed areas quickly with paper table cloths, fabric, or poster board.

Keep captions short in order to get the attention of viewers and to avoid buying or cutting dozens of letters. Investigate craft shops, office supply centers, or teaching materials stores for die-cut, pin-back, and self-adhesive letters. Check with local schools or resource centers for use of an Ellison machine, which cuts several letters at once.

Add three dimensional items for special interest and place a border around the edge to give a finished look.

Consider a rotating schedule for bulletin board responsibility or designate one person to coordinate displays. Plan to change designs about once a month! A "rule of thumb" suggests that after viewing a bulletin board on five or six different occasions, people no longer notice it.

Five "sense-ational" bulletin boards featuring the themes of sight, smell, sound, taste, and touch are suggested for use during Advent, Christmas, and Epiphany. In church facilities and school buildings, as well as in family homes and retirement communities, they can be created in hallways, classrooms, offices, and anywhere there is a surface on which to mount a display.

Sight: Inspirational Bulletin Board

Make use of beautiful Christmas cards, pictures from curriculum packets, or old issues of magazines for a simple and inspirational bulletin board. Reproductions of paintings by famous artists are excellent for a religious holiday theme.

Cover the background with velvet fabric for a look of elegance. Mount larger pictures on gold paper lace place mats or frame the pictures with wide gold ribbon. Pictures from greeting cards can be mounted on gold lace doilies to resemble ornaments or medallions. Allow ample space for a caption, scripture reference, and border. Do not place pictures too close together so the beauty of each one can be appreciated separately.

Choose a caption that relates to the theme of the pictures featured. Write "See His Star" if most of the illustrations include stars, Bethlehem, and wise ones. "Behold, I bring you Good News" would be appropriate for pictures of the Holy Family, angels, and shepherds. Frame the display with wide gold ribbon.

Smell: "Christmas Smells Like ..." Graffiti Board

Cover a bulletin board with white paper. Arrange a garland of real or artificial evergreens around the frame. Real greens will smell great, but might shed. Attach small wrapped peppermint candies or candy canes for color as well as for a sweet scent or treat.

Cut or purchase three or four inch red letters for the caption: "Christmas Smells Like ...." Use a long red ribbon to tie on a red marking pen. Invite everyone to write Christmas "smell" memories on this graffiti board. Top off the board with a big red bow.

Sound: "Make a Joyful Noise unto the Lord"

Cover a bulletin board with red fabric or paper. Form artificial evergreens into a wreath, then fasten securely to the center portion of the board. Decorate the evergreens with musical instrument ornaments. Instruments are available in several sizes wherever Christmas decorations are sold.

Use the scripture phrase from Psalm 100: "Make a Joyful Noise unto the Lord ..." as the caption. Position the verse in the center of the wreath, directly on the red paper or on a separate sheet of paper. Use a marker with a wide tip, a calligraphy pen, or small cut out letters to print the words. Cut small musical notes from construction paper for a border or to scatter in the open areas.

This bulletin board design could be a perfect backdrop for announcements of church musical events or community concerts. If it is used in that way, make the wreath smaller and staple the announcements around the edges.

Taste: Recipe Exchange

Cover a bulletin board with a red and white checkered tablecloth or one with a Christmas design. In the center of the cover, fasten a table setting: large white, red, or green paper plate; paper cup; plastic knife, spoon, and fork; and holiday napkin. Use long dressmaker pins or corsage pins to attach items that cannot be stapled.

Print or cut letters for "Holiday Favorites" or "A Taste of Christmas" with a subtitle: "Recipe Exchange." Place a table for supplies under the bulletin board. Provide a basket of index cards, pens, pencils, and tacks. Invite folks to write out a "family favorite" recipe, sign their names, and add to the display. When the bulletin board fills up with a variety of recipes, gather the cards, duplicate them, and make copies available to share on the supply table.

For a true "Taste of Christmas," plan to have samples of the goodies as well a recipes available at a special holiday event!

Touch: Christmas Story in Texture

So many times at displays or exhibits people are told "Do Not Touch!" For this bulletin board, experiment with a tactile display that encourages everyone to "Please Touch!" Cover the board with light or dark blue paper. In the center, staple a picture of a traditional Holy Family—Mary, Joseph, Baby Jesus, Angels, Shepherds, Wise Ones, and animals.

Create a random collage, or crazy quilt, of textures surrounding the picture. Choose textures that relate to the Christmas story: feathers for angels; soft blanket for the Baby Jesus; rough fabric for the clothing of Joseph and the shepherds; fleece or wool for the sheep; straw or hay and wood for the crib; satins, brocades, velvets, and jewels for the kings.

If the participants will be working on this display, read the Christmas story and ask them to think of different types of materials to connect with the animals or people mentioned in the narrative. Each person may select and add a fabric or textured item for the display. Use duct tape or staples to fasten materials so that there are no sharp points to injure exploring fingers!

The collage will have a balanced look if materials, colors, and textures are repeated across the board. Add the words, "Please Touch!" Place the caption under the bulletin board frame or write the words on a band of wide ribbon and fasten it diagonally across one corner.

Game

Riddle Me!

Riddle Me! is a popular game that invites learners to work together to create and solve word puzzles. To play this guessing game, one person is the riddler while another or several others try to guess the sight, smell, sound, taste, and touch of Advent, Christmas, or Epiphany that the riddler has in mind. Guessing can go on until someone identifies the actual image or a limit on the number of guesses can be set. If the riddler succeeds in stumping the riddlees, then he or she gets to continue with another riddle. If one of the players guesses the object of the riddle, that person gets to be the next riddler. The idea is to experience and celebrate as many senses of the seasons as possible.

Sight

Riddle me, riddle me, riddle me ree

Christmas is something that you can see!

[And its color (or shape) is ...? (Suggest a color or shape.)]

[For example ... It's color is green.]

[Answer: Christmas tree.]

Smell

Riddle me, riddle me, riddle me round

Christmas is something that makes a sound!

[And it sounds like ...? (Make a noise.)]

[For example ... Ding, ding, ding, ding.]

[Answer: Sleigh bells.]

Sound

Riddle me, riddle me, riddle me riff

Christmas is something that you can sniff!

[And it smells like ...? (Suggest a scent.)]

[For example ... It smells like vanilla.]

[Answer: Christmas cookies.]

Taste

Riddle me, riddle me, riddle me reel

Christmas is something that you can feel!

[And it feels like ...? (Suggest a touch.)]

[For example ... It feels prickly.]

[Answer: Evergreen.]

Touch

Riddle me, riddle me, riddle me raste

Christmas is something that you can taste!

[And it tastes like ...? (Suggest a flavor.)]

[For example ... It tastes like peppermint.]

[Answer: Candy cane.]

Music

Sensing Christmas Carols

Singing carols is one thing; sensing them is another! Try a variety of activities to accentuate the sights, smells, sounds, tastes, and touches associated with the words and music of the songs of Advent, Christmas, and Epiphany. Use the ideas in faith formation classes, for youth group meetings, at adult education gatherings, and during intergenerational events. In addition, select several to do at home as a family.

Sight

Capture the concept contained in the carol by photographing modern day scenes related to it.

Construct mobiles that depict hymn stories.

Draw scenes from different carols on windows for others to see.

View paintings from various periods of art and match one with each carol.

Smell

Develop a game listing ten carols on the left side of the paper and ten smells on the right side of the sheet. Match the answers.

Prepare bags with scents suggested in carols and guess the smells associated with the song.

Purchase scratch 'n sniff stickers and match one with each carol.

Write a guided meditation based on the words of a carol and incorporate various smells into the script.

Sound

Attend a concert, in person or virtually, and listen to the music of the season.

Challenge participants to "Name That Tune."

Read the story of a carol before or after singing it.

Simulate sound effects to match the lyrics.

Taste

Bake bread and remember that Bethlehem means "city of bread."

Get a taste of different types of music by playing carols performed by various groups.

Match a different feeling or mood with each carol and journal about a taste of love, joy, peace, and so forth.

Taste foods from the country where the carol originated, or from the period of history to which it refers.

Touch

Arrange an assortment of objects, create a worship center, and encourage people to touch the display!

Create a collage—small or large, individual or group.

Form a three dimensional bulletin board related to one or more carols.

Make books about carols and put a different texture on each page. Give the completed projects to young children or to people with impaired vision.

CHRISTMAS PAGEANT

The Menagerie at the Manger

Critters around the Crèche is intended to be used in conjunction with the resource *The Menagerie at the Manger: Children's Christmas Pageant.* While *Critters* provides weekly scripture stories and faith formation activities for use in congregations, homes, and schools, *Menagerie* offers materials to develop and present a program on the same themes of the animals and the senses. In both cases, music is an integral part of the stories shared in classes and services on Sundays, throughout the week with families, and at a presentation for the community.

Theme Song

"Light the Advent Candles," an original song sung to the tune "Go, Tell It on the Mountain," is used as the theme song for both *Critters* and *Menagerie.* It is sung at the conclusion of the weekly scripture story in church and at home and also used at the end of every scene of the pageant. Although there are six verses, plus the chorus, five stanzas are incorporated into the pageant while six are used with the scripture stories. All verses and the chorus highlight the animal, the sense, and the lesson for the week.

Anthems

Two anthems are included in the *Menagerie* pageant, one sung during the gathering and the other at the conclusion of the program:

- "Sweet Little Jesus Boy"
- "The Friendly Beasts."

If a pageant will be held, take time to prepare the anthems during class each week. If a program is not planned, the students will still enjoy learning and singing these songs. In addition to the music and the words, a hymn story is provided for each anthem which shares the background of the carol and suggests a teaching tool to reinforce the message.

Carols

Four familiar seasonal songs are highlighted in both resources. They are suggested as the carol for each week's scripture story in *Critters* and they are included as the songs sung by the audience in *Menagerie.* They are:

- "Away in a Manger"
- "Good Christian Friends, Rejoice"
- "Joy to the World"
- "O Come, All Ye Faithful".

Music for all four carols is readily available in hymn books, as well as at many online sites. As an engaging way to share the songs with the learners during the weeks of Advent, Christmas, and Epiphany, hymn stories are provided. In addition to learning about the timeless carols, participants will come to understand their timely messages by hearing the back stories and using the activities.

Accompaniment

Accompaniment for the music may be provided on guitar, a variety of instruments, keyboard, organ, and/or piano.

THEME SONG

"Light the Advent Candles"

Tune: "Go, Tell It on the Mountain" • Lyrics: Anna L. Liechty and Phyllis Vos Wezeman

Verse One [Scene One: Hear Love!]

The donkey starts our journey
to Bethlehem to hear
the news the people long for
that Christ is drawing near.

Chorus [Verse One—Verse Four]

Light the Advent candles!
Let them burn brightly far and near!
Sending out their message
that Jesus will soon be here!

Verse Two [Scene Two: Smell Hope!]

The dog can sense the fragrance
of hope that's in the air
expectantly awaiting
God's Christmas joy to share.

Verse Three [Scene Three: Taste Peace!]

The dove within its mouth holds
the olive branch of peace.
And everyone who's hungry
is invited to God's feast.

Verse Four [Scene Four: Touch Joy!]

The cow provides her warmth for
the baby from above.
The hay holds baby Jesus
who touches hearts with love.

Verse Five [Scene Five: See Light!]

The sheep kneels at the manger
and bows his horns so curled
to see the Lamb of God who's
the Savior of the world.

Chorus [Verse Five]

Light the Christmas candle!
Let it burn brightly far and near!
Sending out the message
that Jesus Christ is here.

Light the Advent Candles

Sung to the tune of "Go, Tell It on the Mountain"

Lyrics: Anna L. Liechty and Phyllis Vos Wezeman

ANTHEM

"Sweet Little Jesus Boy"

Music and lyrics by Robert MacGimsey

Music scores for this Christmas spiritual are available from a variety of publishers, including Hope Publishing. Many performances of the song can be found on YouTube.

ANTHEM

"The Friendly Beasts"

Tune: Orientis Partibus • Lyrics: Robert Davis

Verse One

Jesus, our brother, strong and good,
was humbly born in a stable rude,
and the friendly beasts around him stood,
Jesus, our brother, strong and good.

Verse Two

"I," said the donkey, shaggy and brown,
"I carried his mother uphill and down,
I carried his mother to Bethlehem town;
I," said the donkey, shaggy and brown.

Verse Three

"I," said the cow, all white and red,
"I gave him my manger for his bed,
I gave him hay to pillow His head;
I," said the cow, all white and red.

Verse Four

"I," said the sheep with curly horn,
"I gave him my wool for his blanket warm,
He wore my coat on Christmas morn;
I," said the sheep with curly horn.

Verse Five

"I," said the dove, from the rafters high,
"I cooed Him to sleep that he should not cry,
we cooed Him to sleep, my mate and I;
I," said the dove, from the rafters high.

Verse Six

Thus all the beasts, by some good spell,
in the stable dark were glad to tell
of the gifts they gave Emmanuel,
the gifts they gave Emmanuel.

Find free sheet music at http://bit.ly/friendly-beasts

HYMN STORIES

Introduction

There are many resources that trace the stories behind the hymns we sing in worship, yet most parishioners have not heard them and certainly children and youth are unaware of them. Since music is the basis for much of our faith and songs are an integral part of our services, learning about hymns seems a logical place to derive ideas for children's lessons and stories.

The basis for the hymn stories provided—for carols connected with the lessons in *Critters* and for the music in the *Menagerie* pageant—is a design for a children's message using an object lesson related to a familiar hymn text. A unique part of these stories is that directions for making the object are provided with the intent that the teaching tool also be used as a learning activity in faith formation classes, worship services, or family activities. Included are directions for creating the teaching tool, a suggested script, and instructions for leaders. To reinforce the message, each learner may be given directions for creating the story-related object either at church, school, or home. Of course, to best connect the lesson with the words of each hymn, the song should be sung in worship, in classes, or at home.

The following is a suggested script for introducing the concept of a hymn story:

> *[Hold up a hymnal or refer to words of a song on a screen.]*
>
> What is this?
>
> *[Give the children time to answer.]*
>
> This is a book of hymns—a volume of songs we sing to praise and worship God.
>
> Did you ever think about how a book like this gets started? Each of the hymns in this book is a story because each hymn was written by a person trying to tell his or her story of faith. Over the years these hymns became a part of our church's story. Maybe you have a favorite song that you like to sing—and that way hymns become our stories of faith, too. What we are going to do together is to look at some of the hymns we sing, maybe learn some new ones, and find out the story behind them.

Hymn stories invite all ages to hear the message of faith behind the words we often sing. More than just hearing, however, participants can become involved in creative experiences that celebrate both the people whose hymns we share and the God whose name we praise.

HYMN STORY

"Away in a Manger"

Background Information

- Composer: Attributed to Martin Luther; Verses 1 and 2, Anonymous (1885); Verse 3, John Thomas McFarland (1851-1913)
- Year of Publication: 1887 (Murray Tune)
- Tune: MUELLER
- Scripture Reference: Luke 2:7

Theme

Jesus' love surrounds us yesterday, today, and tomorrow.

Teaching Tool: Manger Ornament

Materials

- Craft sticks—three per project
- Christmas cards with manger scenes
- Glue
- Marker, permanent
- Scissors
- Yarn

Method

Cut a manger scene, approximately two-inches by three-inches, from a used Christmas card. Form a triangular-shaped frame around the picture by gluing one craft stick across the bottom and one on each side of the picture. Tie a piece of yarn around the top of the sticks to use as a hanger for the ornament. Using permanent marker, write one of these words on each stick: Past, Present, Future.

Suggestions for Dialogue and Discussion

What is the first Christmas carol you ever learned?

[Children may suggest "Silent Night" but "Away in a Manger" should come up.]

Did you know one of those simple children's carols has a very confusing history? "Away in a Manger" is a simple carol, but to try to discover where the song came from can be very difficult. For many years people believed that the song was written by Martin Luther as a lullaby to sing to his children. But people who research such things say that is not possible. The carol first appeared around 1885 as a lullaby; then two years later James Ramsey Murray published it, with the tune we sing today, in his collection of hymns for children, but only with the first two verses. Some say the third verse was found as early as 1892. Others say Dr. John T. McFarland wrote the third stanza as a favor for his Methodist Bishop friend in the early 1900s. So who knows? The story the song tells, however, is really very simple.

The first stanza of the carol tells a story from the past. Can you remember what that story is?

[Allow children to respond or prompt them with the first line of the carol.]

Yes, the first verse is based on the Christmas story found in the Bible in Luke, chapter 2, verse 7. Jesus did arrive as a baby, just like you and me. And that happened a long time ago.

[Hold up the example and point to the word "past."]

But the second verse is about the present—today! The second part of the verse is really a prayer: "Be near me Lord Jesus" ... can you finish it?

[Invite children to complete the prayer.]

That prayer is for us in the present.

[Hold up the example and point to the word "present."]

The third verse—the one added later—is really about the future. Although Jesus came to earth as a baby, he didn't stay small. He grew up and became our Lord and Savior—the One who will be with us always, both now and later in heaven.

[Hold up the example and point to the word "future."]

No matter who wrote "Away in a Manger," no matter where it came from, it is still one of the most popular Christmas carols in the world, and its simple message reminds us that Jesus' love surrounds us yesterday, today, and tomorrow. And, that's what's important to remember.

"Good Christian Friends, Rejoice!"

Background Information

- Composer: 14th century Latin carol
- Year of Publication: Before 1400
- Tune: In Dulci Jubilo based on traditional German melody
- Scripture Reference: Isaiah 49:13

Theme

The joyous news of Christ's birth moves us to celebrate.

Teaching Tool: Interpretive Movement

Materials

- Marker
- Poster board

Method

Since a Christmas carol is meant to be danced, learn interpretative movement to accompany the story of "Good Christian Friends, Rejoice!" Write the words and movements on poster board to share with the group.

Good Christian friends

[Side step right. Slide left foot and bring feet together.]

Rejoice

[Side step left. Slide right foot to bring feet together.]

With heart and soul and voice;

[Repeat side steps.]

Give ye heed to what we say:

[Take four steps forward.]

Jesus Christ is born today.

[Take four steps backward.]

Ox and ass before him bow,

[Bow from waist.]

And he is in the manger now.

[Extend hands and arms forward.]

Christ is born today! Christ is born today!

[Join hands and lift arms. Repeat side steps right and left.]

Suggestions for Dialogue and Discussion

First, everyone sit very, very still. Don't move a muscle!

[Gain everyone's cooperation, if possible.]

Now that you are sitting very, very still, I want you to imagine the happiest day of your life! Think of having a good time; think of celebrating. Now don't move! Are you picturing yourself being happy? Tell me, when you picture yourself being happy is it hard to sit still?

[Wait for responses.]

Okay, you can quit being quite so still. Isn't it hard to think of a joyous celebration and not want to move around? Isn't Christmas one of the most joyous celebrations we have as Christians? Of course it is! And joy makes us want to move!

Now you are ready to understand the difference between a Christmas song or hymn and a Christmas "carol." A carol is a tune that can be danced! Early tunes for Christmas carols or dances usually came from folk melodies that were used for local festivals and celebrations. "Good Christian Friends, Rejoice" is a good example of an early Christmas carol that was based on a German folk tune. The first records of the carol are written with both German and Latin phrases together. Later it was translated into English. The Latin tune "In Dulci Jubilo" means "sweet shouting." The English words challenge us to rejoice with "heart, and soul, and voice." The best way to do that is to dance and sing! Let me teach you some simple steps we can do together as good Christian friends rejoicing!

[Teach movement as explained in the instructions.]

Dance is a universal language. A Christmas carol is truly meant to call us to celebrate the joy of Christ's birth with our whole being. "Good Christian Friends, Rejoice" reminds us why we are celebrating Christ's birth—Christ was born to save! That should put a spring in our step everyday!

"Joy to the World"

Background Information

- Composer: Isaac Watts (1674-1748)
- Year of Publication: 1719
- Tune: ANTIOCH by Lowell Mason based on Handel's *Messiah*
- Scripture Reference: Psalm 98

Theme

God's gift of salvation brings joy to the world.

Teaching Tool: Świąt/World (Polish paper ornament)

Materials

- Embroidery needle
- Paper, construction, foil, or poster board
- Scissors
- Thread

Method

Because of its many sections and its spherical shape, the Polish ornament known as the Świąt is commonly called the world. Cut three equal circles from construction paper, foil, or poster board. They may be the same or different colors. Follow the illustrations and cut the indicated lines on each circle. Write the following words on each circle:

- Circle A: Joy to the ... / World / Isaac / Watts
- Circle B: Messiah / George / Frederick / Handel
- Circle C: Antioch / Lowell / Mason / American.

Fold circle A in half and insert it through the center slot of circle B. Unfold A. Fold A and B so that the cut slots line up. Insert the two folded circles through C. Unfold the circles and arrange them to form a ball.

Make a hanger for the ornament. Thread an embroidery needle and bring the needle and thread through the edge of one of the circles. Knot the loop and cut off the thread. The ornament is ready to place on the tree.

Suggestions for Dialogue and Discussion

How do you spell joy? I'll give you a hint: there are three letters just like the three circles.

[Hold up the three circles.]

J-O-Y spells "joy!" What does joy mean?

[Probably most will suggest happiness. Add the idea that surprise is often a part of our joy.]

Can you think of a famous carol we sing about joy at Christmastime?

[They should be able to guess "Joy to the World."]

"Joy to the World" is indeed one of the most famous Christmas carols we sing, written by Isaac Watts.

[Hold up the circle with his name.]

You might be surprised to learn that Isaac Watts didn't write this song as a Christmas song! It was his interpretation of Psalm 98 in praise of God's goodness and power. Isaac Watts didn't have a lot in his life to be joyful about: he was often sick, he was so small and homely no one wanted to marry him, and he had to live as a guest in a friend's home for 36 years because he wasn't able to work and support himself. That does not sound like a very happy life, does it? However, Isaac Watts had discovered a source for joy in his life: God's presence! Like the Psalms celebrate the power and glory of God, "Joy to the World" celebrates God's coming to earth in the form of Jesus to bring hope to all the world.

At the same time Isaac Watts lived in London, so did another great man named George Frederick Handel.

[Hold up the circle with his name.]

He wrote his music to the glory of God, so he knew about the joy of God's presence, too. One night, after prayer, he rose to begin his most famous work *Messiah*, and he composed all 53 musical numbers in just 23 days. Although Isaac Watts and George Frederick Handel probably knew each other, it was almost 100 years later in America before Handel's music and Watts' words were put together.

[Insert the first circle into the second.]

An American named Lowell Mason was a choir director and a public school teacher. He adapted Handel's music for churches to use in worship in a tune now called "Antioch," and combined it with the words of Isaac Watts, renaming the new song "Joy to the World." So it took three gifted people nearly 100 years to put together what is now one of the world's favorite Christmas carols.

[Add the third circle to the ornament, as directed.]

Our last circle creates a paper world called a "Święt," which is a Polish Christmas ornament. That's surprising, isn't it? We can create a three dimensional ball out of three flat pieces of paper.

It's surprising, too, that God could bring together the talents of three people to create this beautiful song. Of course, it is also surprising that God sent a baby to bring the gift of salvation, which is the true joy for all the world. Our three musicians knew that—and now so do we.

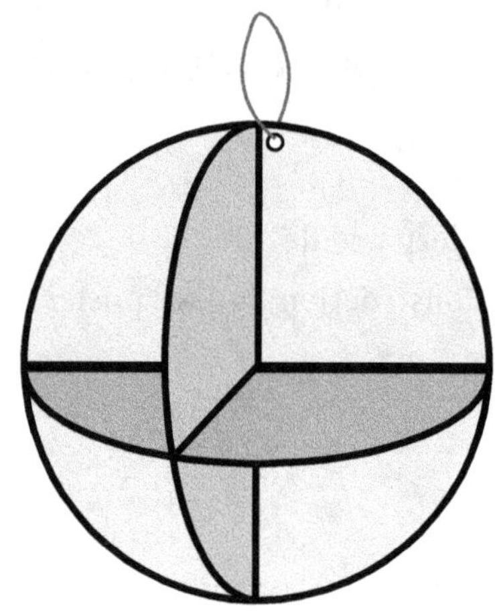

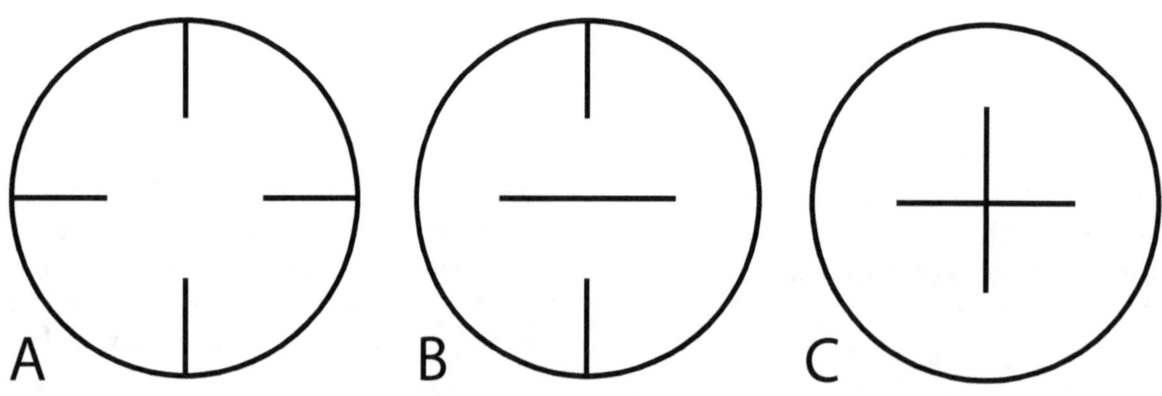

"O, Come, All Ye Faithful"

Background information

- Composer: John Francis Wade (1711-1786)
- Translator: Frederick Oakeley (1802-1880)
- Year of Publication: 1743
- Tune: THE PORTUGUESE HYMN
- Scripture Reference: Luke 2:15, 20

Theme

The faithful respond to the invitation to adore the Lord.

Teaching Tool: Footprint Shape Book

Materials

- Hole punch
- Markers
- Paper, construction
- Pencil
- Ribbon or yarn
- Scissors

Method

Cut five pieces of construction paper into footprint shapes. Although they may be any color, they should be the same size. Punch a hole in the center of the heel of each shape. Bind the pages together by tying them with a length of ribbon or yarn. Write the following words on the footprints:

Footprint One

- Front—Blank
- Back—Adeste Fideles

Footprint Two

- Front—O Come, All Ye Faithful
- Back—John Francis Wade; France

Footprint Three

- Front—Frederick Oakeley; England
- Back: O Come, All Ye Faithful

Footprint Four

- Front—How Firm a Foundation
- Back—O Come

Footprint Five

- Front—Let Us Adore Him
- Back—Blank

Suggestions for Dialogue and Discussion

Like footprints, much of the information about "O Come, All Ye Faithful" comes in pairs.

[Hold up the shape book and open to the first two footprints.]

This hymn was first written in Latin and was known by its Latin name, "Adeste Fideles," which means be present or near, ye faithful, or "O Come, All Ye Faithful."

[Turn to the next set of footprints.]

John Francis Wade is believed to be the person who wrote or found the words and music to this much-loved hymn. He made his living by hand copying music for churches, since that was before copy machines. Although many church hymnals list the composer of this hymn as anonymous—meaning no one knows who wrote it—researchers feel confident that John

Wade was the first person to share "Adeste Fideles" with other Christians in France.

Many years later, Frederick Oakeley—impressed with the Latin words—decided to translate their meaning into English for his Anglican congregation to sing. The first translation he made began "Ye Faithful, Approach Ye." Later, he studied the Latin more carefully and improved his translation to the words we sing today.

[Turn to the next set of footprint pages.]

Not only were two men responsible for bringing the world this great hymn in two languages; but in the church today, the Portuguese Hymn provides the music for two great hymns: "O Come, All Ye Faithful" and "How Firm a Foundation."

[Turn to the last pair of footprints.]

This hymn challenges Christians to come to Bethlehem, but it also gives us further instructions: we are to adore the Christ child. To be faithful, we must do both. Our footprints symbolize our coming to stand before the Christ, but we come for a purpose—to offer our devotion and love to the newborn King.

In Advent, as we wait for the Christ Child's birth, we must make sure our footsteps are leading us toward the manger, toward Bethlehem, toward the One whom we adore.

HYMN STORY

"Sweet Little Jesus Boy"

Background Information

- Composer: Robert MacGimsey (1898-1979)
- Year of Publication: 1934
- Tune: ROBERT MACGIMSEY
- Scripture Reference: John 8:12

Theme

Seeing Jesus in the manger lights our understanding and our world.

Teaching Tool: Sleep Mask

Materials

- Copy machine or printer
- Fabric such as felt or fleece with design of music notes, if possible
- Hole punch
- Marker, fine-point permanent
- Paper for printer
- Pencil
- Ribbon, 1/4 inch wide
- Scissors

Method

Duplicate the pattern for the mask. Cut out the shape. Use a pencil to trace the mask pattern on a piece of felt or fleece.

Punch, or use a scissor point to poke, a hole on each side of the mask, approximately one-half inch from the edge.

Cut two pieces of ribbon into 12-inch lengths. Use a fine-point permanent marker to print the following words on each of the ribbons:

- Ribbon One—"Sweet Little Jesus Boy"
- Ribbon Two—Robert MacGimsey.

While sharing the hymn story, the ribbon with the name of the author will be tied through the hole on one side of the mask and the ribbon with the name of the hymn will be attached through the hole on the other side of the mask.

Suggestions for Dialogue and Discussion

Have you ever had trouble going to sleep? Maybe on Christmas Eve? It's like our eyes don't want to stay closed, right?

[Wait for responses.]

What if we made a mask to wear so that we could sleep as soundly as Baby Jesus? That might be helpful on Christmas Eve.

[Hold up mask without eye holes or ribbons.]

Putting on a mask can help us remember that sometimes—even when we are wide awake, wearing no mask—we still do not see. This mask will help us learn a story about a Christmas song that was written during a time like that—a time when people really didn't see clearly about how they were treating one another. The song is "Sweet Little Jesus Boy."

[Hold up the ribbon with the title, read the name of the song, and tie the ribbon through the hole on one side of the mask.]

Once in America, in the early part of the twentieth century, a young man named Robert MacGimsey was growing up on a plantation in Louisiana. Slavery had ended many years before, but African American people still didn't have equal opportunity and equal rights.

[Hold up the second ribbon, read his name, and tie it to the second hole on the mask.]

Robert's parents employed many African American descendants of slaves and their son grew up being cared for by the people others seemed not to see. Robert especially loved his nanny, "Aunt Becky." He liked listening to the spirituals she sang when she rocked him to sleep. As he grew older, Robert sang spirituals in church with his "uncles"—the term he used to show respect to the African American men who were his mentors. Robert could see and value the people and the music that were part of his life.

[Show the ribbon with his name again.]

Although Robert became a lawyer like his father, he loved music most of all, and his mother made sure her son also studied music composition at Julliard in New York. Robert worked to record and write the music of African American communities to preserve the tunes and lyrics, as well as the names of the people who taught them to him or recorded them for him.

{Point to the music notes on the fabric.]

One Christmas Robert was sad to see that people seemed to celebrate without honoring the birth of the Savior. He felt the people who couldn't see that Christmas was about Baby Jesus were like the folks who didn't see who people really were because of the color of their skin.

When Robert MacGimsey wrote his most famous song "Sweet Little Jesus Boy," he wanted it to sound like the songs he enjoyed in his childhood. In fact, many people assumed "Sweet Little Jesus Boy" was an African American spiritual written from the time of slavery. Robert felt that if we could just see, we could choose to treat Jesus—and one another—in a way that shows God's love.

It's important to tell Robert MacGimsey's story and listen carefully to the words he wants us to sing like a loving lullaby. This Christmas let's only use our masks to sleep. The rest of the time we can wake up to the light of God's love—for ourselves and for our world.

[Hold up completed mask.]

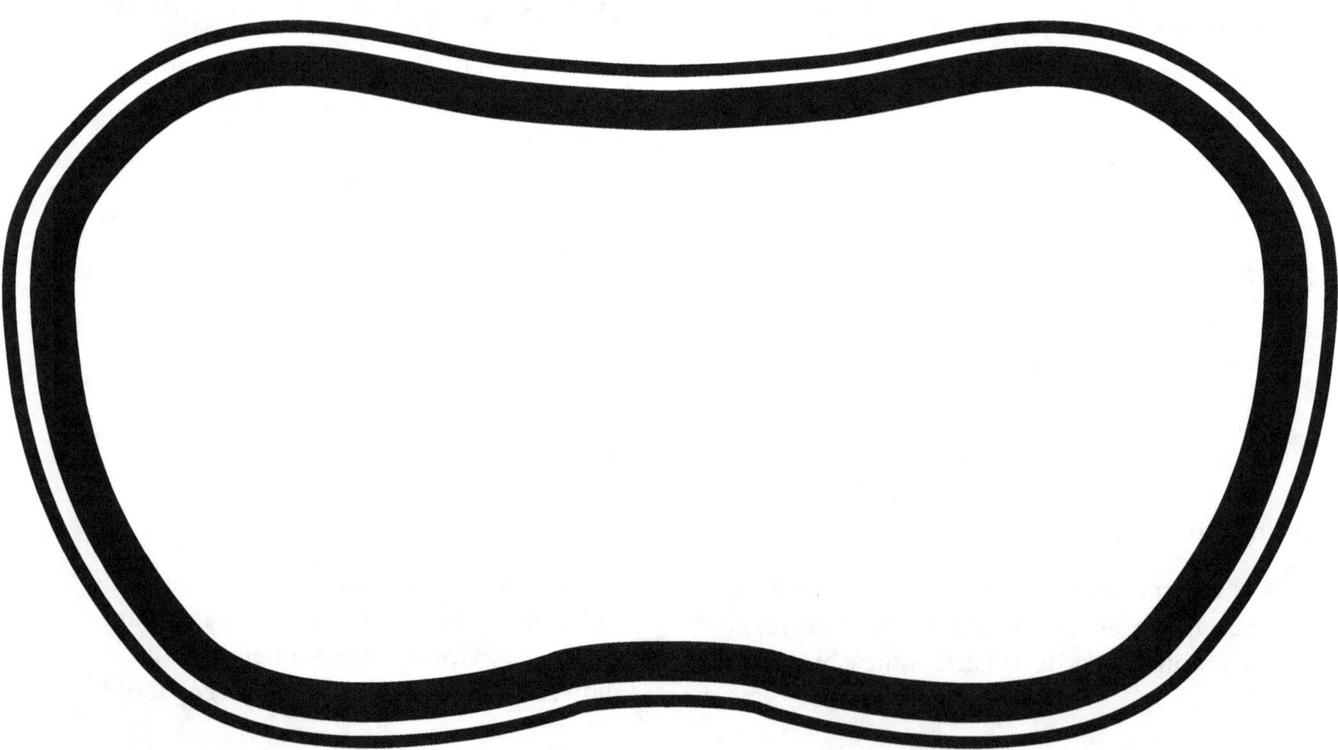

"The Friendly Beasts"

Background Information

- Composer: Robert Davis (1881-1950)
- Year of Publication: 1920s, 1934
- Tune: ORIENTIS PARTIBUS, 12th Century French Carol
- Scripture Reference: Matthew 5:8

Theme

We worship Jesus, our newborn Savior, with the greatest gift we have to bring—ourselves.

Teaching Tool: Gift Box of Gifts

Materials

- Bag, plastic
- Copy machine or printer
- Gift boxes with removable lids—1 large and 4 small (the 4 must fit inside the large box)
- Glue (Optional)
- Markers
- Paper for copy machine or printer—red
- Patterns for Animals—Cow, Donkey, Dove, Lamb/Sheep [See "Learning the Story" section] (optional)
- Resource Sheet: Pattern for Heart
- Ribbon (optional)
- Scissors (optional)

Method

Prepare the five boxes to use while sharing the hymn story. One box must be large enough to hold the other four. The four smaller boxes may be the same or different sizes.

On the top of the lid of the largest box, print the title of the hymn, "The Friendly Beasts." On one side, write the name of the composer, Robert Davis, and the year of publication, 1934.

On the top of each of the smaller four boxes, print the name of one of the animals mentioned in the song—donkey, cow, sheep, dove—or glue a cutout shape of the animal on the lid.

Prepare hearts for the boxes and for the participants. Duplicate the heart pattern on red paper and cut out the shapes. On each of four hearts, print the following words: Cow—Manger, Donkey—Ride, Dove—Coo, and Sheep—Wool. Place each of these hearts in the corresponding animal's box. If desired, tie each box with ribbon to make it look more festive.

Place the four prepared boxes inside the larger box.

Put the rest of the red hearts in a plastic bag and set them inside the large box as well. They will be distributed to the participants at the end of the hymn story.

Suggestions for Dialogue and Discussion

Who here loves animals? Do any of you have pets?

[Allow the participants to name favorite animals and pets.]

Animals bring many gifts to our lives, don't they? Maybe that's why favorite Christmas stories often include the stable animals that must have been present when Jesus was born. In fact, one of the earliest Christmas hymns sung to teach everyone about the birth of Jesus is called "The Friendly Beasts."

[Hold up the large box and point to the title of the hymn.]

The words we sing today were written by Robert Davis and first published in 1934.

[Turn the box to show the information.]

But the song itself is very old, dating back almost 1,000 years when most people could not read the story of Jesus birth for themselves.

The donkey was one of the first stable animals church leaders in France used to tell the story of Jesus' birth. They would lead a procession through the village to the church to act out Mary's arrival in Bethlehem. Our song tells us about a gift the donkey gave to baby Jesus.

[Open the large box, take out the donkey's gift, and ask a child to hold it until asked to open it.]

As the song and the celebration became more popular the people in England added more verses and more animals. A cow, a sheep, and a dove each provided a gift to the baby Jesus, adding more verses to the song "The Friendly Beasts."

Who were the gifts for?

[Baby Jesus!]

That's right! And each animal gave a different one.

[Distribute the gifts for the cow, the sheep, and the dove to different children and instruct them to hold the boxes until asked to open them.]

Let's open the boxes, one at a time, and see what each animal's gift is to baby Jesus.

What did the donkey give?

[Ask the child holding the donkey box to open it, take out the gift—which is a heart—and read the word "ride."]

The donkey's gift is a ride for Mary!

What did the sheep give?

[Ask the child holding the sheep's box to open it, take out the gift—which is a heart—and read the word "wool."]

The sheep gave her own wool for warmth!

Now the cow.

[Ask the child holding the cow's box to open it, take out the gift—which is a heart—and read the word "manger."]

The cow's gift is a manger bed!

And finally, the dove.

[Ask the child holding the dove's box to open it, take out the gift—which is a heart—and read the word "coo."]

The dove cooed a lullaby!

Those were the best gifts because they were gifts from where?

[They were gifts from the heart!]

As we sing "The Friendly Beasts" this Christmas season, let's be reminded that just reading about the birth of Jesus is not enough. We need to put ourselves in the story. We need to offer the one special gift we each can bring – our own lives ... and our own hearts.

[Distribute a paper heart to each participant.]

Snacks

Animal-Themed Treats

In keeping with the theme of *Critters around the Crèche*, enjoy animal themed treats as refreshments at events, snacks in class, and desserts at home. These recipes can be made in advance and ready-to-serve during a lesson or a social. They may also be created by people of all ages and used as a cooperative project during family time and intergenerational gatherings. Besides the snacks suggested there are many more that could be made; check the internet for additional ideas.

While the ingredients, supplies, and instructions provided are a guide for preparing the snacks, additional supplies such as plates, napkins, and forks may be needed to serve them. In addition, if drinks are offered with the treats, beverages and cups are required.

Of course, with any food project, be sure to sanitize the work space at the beginning and the end of the session. Provide clean up supplies for the participants so they may wash and dry their hands throughout the process as well.

Donkey Face No Bake Cookies

Ingredients [24 Cookies]

- Candy eyes, 24
- Cookies: Milano or Nutter Butter, 12 of one variety plus mini vanilla wafers, 12
- Icing tubes—black, brown, white
- Tootsie roll, 1

Supplies

- Kitchen shears
- Plate

Instructions

Create long-faced donkeys from a combination of purchased cookies. While Milano by Pepperidge Farm or Nutter Butter by Nabisco work well for the project, be aware of peanut allergies when deciding which one to use as the face of the donkey.

Begin by setting out twelve mini vanilla wafers. With black icing, draw a smiley face on each of them. A curved line may serve as the mouth and the two dots can become the nostrils. Using a small dab of frosting on the back side, attach a decorated vanilla wafer to the bottom of each Milano or Nutter Butter cookie, following the curve of the base.

Using kitchen shears, cut the Tootsie Roll into thin pieces to use as pointed ears. Roll each piece of candy between fingers to achieve the desired shape. Use a dab of frosting to attach the ears to either side of the top of the cookie head. With brown frosting, add a tuft of hair between the two ears. Finish the face by using frosting to attach two candy eyes to the head. If candy eyes are not available, make two circles with white frosting and add a black dot in the center of each of them.

Place completed donkey faces on a plate.

Puppy Chow without Peanut Butter

Ingredients

- 1/2 cup chocolate chips
- 2 Tablespoons butter
- 1/2 teaspoon vanilla
- 4 1/2 cups Chex™ cereal
- 2/3 cup powdered sugar

Supplies

- Bag, large plastic
- Bowls, large (2) and small (1)
- Measuring cups and spoons
- Microwave oven
- Spoon for mixing

Instructions

Put chocolate chips and butter in a microwave safe bowl. Microwave for one minute and stir until well blended. Add vanilla and stir.

Put cereal into a large bowl. Pour chocolate mix over the cereal and stir.

Once the cereal is coated, and after it is cooled, place the chocolate covered cereal and powered sugar in a bag. Seal the bag securely and shake until well blended.

Pour the mix into a bowl and enjoy the "Puppy Chow."

Dove-Shaped Butter Cookies

Ingredients [18 Cookies]

- 1 stick unsalted butter
- 1/2 cup sugar
- 1/4 teaspoon salt
- 1 large egg
- 1 Tablespoon light corn syrup
- 1 Tablespoon grated lemon zest
- 2 teaspoons vanilla
- 2 1/4 cups all-purpose flour
- Icing tubes—blue, white

Supplies

- Bowl, large
- Cookie cutter(s), dove shaped
- Cookie sheets
- Measuring cups and spoons
- Mixer
- Paper, waxed
- Oven
- Refrigerator
- Rolling pin
- Spatula
- Wire racks

Instructions

In a large bowl beat butter, sugar, and salt with mixer on medium-high speed until light and fluffy, about three minutes. Reduce speed to medium and add egg; beat until combined. Beat in corn syrup, lemon zest, and vanilla. Reduce speed to low and add flour in two batches.

Shape dough into two disks; wrap and refrigerate one hour.

Heat oven to 350° F. Roll out one disk of dough at a time between two sheets of waxed paper to one-fourth inch thickness. Remove top layer of waxed paper and use a dove-shaped cookie cutter to form the shapes. Transfer to a cookie sheet and bake for twelve minutes or until cookies are golden in color. Transfer cookies to a wire rack to cool completely.

To decorate each dove, apply a blue icing dot for an eye. Use white icing to add trims to the shape.

Cow-Shaped Cheese Slices

Ingredients

Cheese slices, several varieties including American, cheddar, co-jack, Muenster, provolone, and Swiss

Supplies

- Cookie cutters, various sizes of cow shapes
- Cutting board(s)
- Plates

Instructions

Use cow shaped cookie cutters to create this dairy farm animal from a selection of cheese slices and serve them as a snack. Place the treats on a cutting board or a plate.

Lamb Layer Cake

Ingredients [One 2-layer cake]

- 1 package white cake mix
- Ingredients for cake mix
- Cooking spray
- 1 8-ounce tub whipped topping, thawed
- 15 large white marshmallows, cut in half
- 1/4 teaspoon pink colored sugar
- 1 pink jelly bean
- 1 tube black decorator gel

Supplies

- Bowl
- Knife
- Measuring cups and spoons
- Mixer
- Oven
- Pans, 2 9-inch round
- Parchment paper
- Plate
- Spatula
- Toothpicks
- Wire racks

Instructions

Heat oven to 350° F.

Cover bottoms of cake pans with parchment paper and coat with cooking spray.

Mix cake batter as directed on package. Pour into prepared pans. Bake for time suggested on box or until toothpick inserted in center comes out clean. Cool cakes in pans for 15 minutes. Invert layers onto wire racks; gently remove pans and parchment paper. Cool cake completely before frosting.

Place one layer on serving plate. Spread with one cup whipped topping. Cover with the second cake layer. Frost top and sides with remaining topping.

Form the face of the lamb on the top of the frosted layer cake. Press cut sides of two marshmallow halves in colored pink sugar. Gently press, colored side up, one marshmallow half into the center of the right side of the cake and the other into the center of the left side of the cake. Outline the entire outer edge of the cake top with a circle of marshmallow halves and place two additional rows across the top to form the lamb's wool. Place a pink jelly bean in the center of the face for the nose. Use black decorator gel to draw a wide "W" shape for the mouth and two lines for eyes.

Camel Fruit Figure

Ingredients [1 Camel]

- Banana, 1
- Blueberries, 18
- Orange, 1 or 3 firm segments
- Strawberries, 3 whole

Supplies

- Knife
- Plate
- Skewers, wooden or long toothpicks

Instructions

Thoroughly clean blueberries and strawberries. Cut the green tops off of the berries.

Before beginning the construction process, approximate the length needed for the skewers and the toothpicks that will be used to join the pieces of fruit and cut them to the desired size.

For body

Join three whole strawberries, top up, by running a wooden skewer through them horizontally.

For legs

Thread four blueberries onto each of four long toothpicks. Insert two skewers of blueberries to the front, bottom side of the first strawberry and the other two skewers to the back, bottom side of the last strawberry. Stand up the shape and adjust as necessary.

For neck

Cut a banana in half. Insert one end of a skewer or long toothpick into the center of the banana and the other end into the center of the first strawberry. Balance the weight, if necessary.

For humps

Cut the remaining piece of the banana in half. Position each portion on either side of the center strawberry and secure the humps in place with toothpicks. For a firmer fruit, use two segments of an orange in place of the bananas.

For head

Attach one firm orange segment to the front top of the banana.

For eyes

Attach two blueberries, one on each side of the orange segment head, for eyes.

Stand the completed camel on a plate.

Living the Story

Family Time

Overview

Critters around the Crèche offers families an opportunity to prepare for Christmas by using an Advent Wreath at home as the focus for activities and devotions. Building on the theme of the animals that might have been with Baby Jesus, Mary, and Joseph during the first Christmas, a new symbol is featured each week which correlates with one of the human senses. As well, family worship suggestions are provided for Sunday devotions including scripture, music, story, and prayer. Six ideas for living out the message complete each week's preparation, building toward Christmas Day and the birth of Christ and continuing through the celebration of Epiphany.

Advent wreaths come in a variety of styles. One common arrangement is a circle of evergreen branches with purple or blue candles for three Sundays, a pink candle as the light of Christ comes closer, and a white candle in the center, lit on Christmas Day.

Critters around the Crèche is based not only on lighting an additional candle each week, but also on highlighting one of the senses and adding an animal symbol to represent the theme. Families may devise the symbols from a variety of sources such as toys, stickers, pictures, and ornaments or simple illustrations can be traced, decorated, and cut out, with the shapes used to add a personal touch to a family's worship center. Instructions for many craft projects and patterns for the animals used in *Critters* are supplied in the "Learning the Story" section of this book.

While one verse of a carol is suggested for each week's devotion, favorite or more familiar songs may be substituted. The stanza provided matches one of the songs sung during "Hearing the Story." In addition, background on this hymn—which may have been shared in church or school—is supplied in this book's "Learning the Story" materials.

Critters around the Crèche challenges family members to use Advent as an opportunity to explore sight, smell, sound, taste, and touch as they experience the true gifts of Christmas: faith, hope, light, love, joy, and peace.

Hear Love!

Animal Symbol

Donkey

Read

Zechariah 9:9

Rejoice greatly, O daughter Zion! Shout aloud, O daughter Jerusalem! Lo, your king comes to you; triumphant and victorious is he, humble and riding on a donkey, on a colt, the foal of a donkey.

Say

As we light the first Advent Candle, we remember to listen and to hear the Good News—God loves us!

[Light the first Advent candle.]

Sing

"O Come, All Ye Faithful"

O come, all ye faithful, joyful and triumphant,
O come ye, O come ye to Bethlehem;
come and behold him born the King of angels.

Refrain

O come let us adore him,
O come, let us adore him,
O come, let us adore him, Christ the Lord.

Say

Why are donkeys so stubborn? Maybe it's because their big ears hear so many sounds that they don't know which way to go, so they just stop. Some people can be like that at Christmas. There are so many holiday sounds they get confused and they just stop listening for the true message of the season. We can learn from the story of the donkey who listened to Joseph's loving voice and carried Mary safely all the way to Bethlehem. During Advent, while we travel toward Christmas, we, too, must listen for God's voice. Like the donkey, we'll recognize the sound of love.

Pray

Dear God, Help us listen and follow in faith as you lead us to Christmas. Amen.

Do This Week

- Attend a Christmas concert and listen to the music of the season.
- Make a jingle bell wreath for the door.
- Read the story of a carol before or after singing it.
- Share a children's Christmas book and add sound effects.
- Visit a zoo or live nativity scene and listen to the sound a donkey makes.
- Write a list of all the Christmas sounds that are heard in a day.

Smell Hope!

Animal Symbol

Dog

Read

Ephesians 5:1-2

Therefore be imitators of God, as beloved children, and live in love, as Christ loved us and gave himself up for us, a fragrant offering and sacrifice to God.

Say

As we light the second Advent Candle, we remember to lift our heads and catch the scent of hope in the Christmas air—God is near!

[Light the second Advent candle.]

Sing

"Away in a Manger"

Away in a manger, no crib for a bed,
the little Lord Jesus laid down his sweet head;
the stars in the heavens looked down
where he lay,
the little Lord Jesus asleep on the hay.

Say

What kinds of smells would have been part of the first Christmas? Maybe there would have been the scent of fresh hay, the stable animals, and the cold night air. Can't you imagine that the shepherds' dogs out in the field might have caught the scent of something "heavenly" right before the angels arrived? Then after the angels appeared to the shepherds, perhaps the shepherds' dogs helped lead the way to the manger, their noses catching the scent of hope that Jesus brought to earth. The dog's nose is much more keen than ours. During Advent, this symbol can remind us to lift our heads toward heaven and follow the fragrance of hope all the way to Bethlehem.

Pray

Dear God, Help us to catch the scent of hope and follow in faith as you lead us to Christmas. Amen.

Do This Week

- Bake dog biscuits for the animal shelter.
- Burn frankincense near your nativity set.
- Create pomander balls made with whole cloves pressed into oranges and give them as Christmas gifts.
- Gather cleaning supplies to give to local agencies who help families start over after a disaster.
- Make a list of your favorite Christmas smells.
- Read a "scratch and sniff" story of Christmas.

Taste Peace!

Animal

Dove

Read

2 Thessalonians 3:16

Now may the Lord of peace himself give you peace at all times in all ways. The Lord be with all of you.

Say

As we light the third Advent candle, we realize that our greatest longing is to taste God's peace.

[Light the third Advent candle.]

Sing

"Sweet Little Jesus Boy"

Sweet little Jesus boy—
They made you be born in a manger.
Sweet little holy child—
We didn't know who you were.
Didn't know you'd come to save us Lord;
to take our sins away.
Our eyes were blind, we could not see -
We didn't know who you were.

Say

What is your favorite Christmas taste? Candy canes? Gingerbread? Homemade fudge? Have you ever eaten so much that you thought you'd never be hungry again? But hunger always returns. There is only one taste we long for that really can satisfy us—the sweet peace that comes from knowing God's presence. Our third Advent symbol, the dove, reminds us of the peace that Christmas brings. Just like the flutter of wings and the gentle song of the dove, the peace God sends with Jesus' birth quiets and satisfies our deepest longings, allowing all the other hungers of life to find their place.

Pray

Dear God, help us to hunger for the taste of peace this Christmas. Amen.

Do This Week

- Bake dove-shaped cookies for family and friends.
- Fast through one or more meals as a reminder to pray for peace.
- Find Christmas cards with pictures of doves and a message of peace.
- Make place mats and write messages of peace to accompany holiday meals.
- Prepare a new Christmas taste treat to share as a peace offering with another.
- Save money by eating at home instead of at a restaurant and contribute to a cause for peace.

Touch Joy!

Animal Symbol

Cow

Read

John 15:11

I have said these things to you so that my joy may be in you, and that your joy may be complete.

Say

As we light the fourth Advent candle, Christmas approaches and we feel the joy of the warmth of God's presence.

[Light the fourth Advent candle.]

Sing

"Good Christian Friends, Rejoice"

Good Christian friends, rejoice
with heart and soul and voice;
give ye heed to what we say:
Jesus Christ was born today.
Ox and ass before him bow,
and he is in the manger now.
Christ is born today!
Christ is born today!

Say

Have you ever been cold? Even in warm climates, like in Bethlehem, the air can be cold at night. Do you suppose the stable was cold when Jesus was born? Possibly a little? Even if it was cold outside, the warm bodies of the animals within would have taken the chill from the air. That's why our fourth symbol of Advent is the cow, the large, warm animal that might have helped Mary keep baby Jesus cozy in the cold air and damp hay. At Christmas, we can make the world a warmer place by offering a touch of warmth and love in Jesus' name.

Pray

Dear God, Touch us with the joy of Christmas so we can touch others in your name. Amen.

Do This Week

- Arrange an assortment of objects as a worship center and encourage people to touch the display.
- Craft a picture of warmth and love using natural materials like evergreen branches for paint brushes.
- Give baby blankets as a mission gift to local helping agencies.
- Hold hands during grace and family prayers.
- Make a hand print present for family Christmas gift exchanges.
- Write out coupons for some loving touches as Christmas gifts like back rubs, manicures, and hugs.

See Light!

Animal Symbol

Lamb

Read

Luke 2:17-20

When they saw this, they made known what had been told them about this child; and all who heard it were amazed at what the shepherds told them. But Mary treasured all these words and pondered them in her heart. The shepherds returned, glorifying and praising God for all they had heard and seen, as it had been told them.

Say

As we light the Christ candle, we see the promise of salvation fulfilled with the birth of the Lamb of God.

[Light the Christ candle.]

Sing

"The Friendly Beasts"

Jesus, our brother, strong and good,
was humbly born in a stable rude,
and the friendly beasts around him stood,
Jesus, our brother, strong and good.

Say

What Christmas sights fill you with joy? Twinkling lights? Sparkling snowflakes? Brightly wrapped packages? These are delightful visions of Christmas, but the shepherds didn't go to Bethlehem to see lights, snow, or wrapped gifts. They longed to feast their eyes on what God had promised. Maybe the shepherds were the first guests at the stable because Jesus is also known as the Lamb of God, a symbol of a pure offering for sin. We know that the Bible tells us the shepherds praised God for what they saw that first Christmas night. This Christmas we, too, can open our eyes to see Jesus, the Lamb of God who takes away the sin of the world.

Pray

Dear God, Give us eyes to see your gift of Jesus this Christmas. Amen.

Do This Week

- Decorate candles with beads or glitter and share them as gifts of light.
- Do a crayon etching to portray the shepherds' visit to the manger.
- Go see a live nativity and pet the woolly sheep.
- Make tissue paper stained glass windows to display or to give as gifts.
- Place luminaria at the entrance and candles in the windows of your home to light the way for the Christ Child.
- Visit a museum or browse a bookstore to view the Christmas story in art.

Follow Faith!

Animal Symbol

Camel

Read

2 Corinthians 5:7

For we walk by faith, not by sight.

Say

As we re-light the Christ candle, we remember that God will lead us beyond what is known and familiar to an exciting adventure called faith.

[Re-light the Christ candle.]

Sing

"Joy to the World"

Joy to the world! The Lord is come:
let earth receive her King;
let ev'ry heart prepare him room,
and heav'n and nature sing,
and heav'n and nature sing,
and heav'n, and heav'n and nature sing.

Say

Who would make such a ridiculous looking animal as a camel? Only God, of course! It may be funny-looking, but the camel is perfectly suited to crossing the waterless, sandy desert. Probably the wise men came riding on camels to find Jesus, so the camel is our symbol for Epiphany. After the holidays we are often in a rush to get back to normal. However, we need to be wise ourselves and remember that the true message of Christmas is to follow in faith where God leads. Living by faith may look silly to other people, but those who are wise know that the adventure of following God only begins with Christmas and lasts throughout the journey we call life.

Pray

Dear God, Thank you for the sense of faith that teaches us to trust you always. Amen.

Do This Week

- Find a new path to a familiar place.
- Make a faith map of your own walk with God so far, tracing the moments where faith has made a difference in your choices.
- Read "The Other Wise Man" by Henry Van Dyke.
- Risk sharing a message of faith with someone new.
- Search for information about camels in books or on the internet.
- Write New Year's Resolutions about ways you will follow God faithfully this year.

Come to Your Senses Reflections

During Advent, as well as throughout Christmas and Epiphany, take time to allow faith to "Come to Your Senses." Starter Suggestions for each sense, as well as each season, are offered for family members to use individually or together. During the four weeks of Advent, the 12 days of Christmas, and the time of Epiphany, read the scripture passage and reflect on or respond to each simple prompt as a way to explore and experience God's love. If appropriate, journal personal thoughts and feelings or share them during a family dinner or a household meeting. Either way, use this guide as an opportunity for quiet reflection on the message of each season.

Listen [Hear]

Scripture: Isaiah 55:3a

Incline your ear, and come to me; listen, so that you may live. I will make with you an everlasting covenant, my steadfast, sure love for David.

Advent

Listen for God during Advent by learning a new way to pray. Instead of closing eyes and folding hands in prayer, leave eyes open and lift palms up during quiet time.

Christmas

Listen for the gift of loving words during the Christmas season. Instead of brushing compliments or praise aside, receive the gifts with humility as blessings from God.

Epiphany

Listen for new ideas with an open mind. Tune in to a Christian radio or television program, or a service on the internet, to hear how God's love is being revealed to the world.

Breathe [Smell]

Scripture: Job 33:4

The spirit of God has made me, and the breath of the Almighty gives me life.

Advent

Continue to learn new attitudes for prayer: while sitting quietly with palms open, breathe in the presence of God and exhale concerns and worries.

Christmas

While hurrying through the celebrations of Christmas, pause to record memories of Christmas in the air: breathe in and savor the seasonal smells outside, in the kitchen, and around the tree.

Epiphany

Fill the season with fragrant offerings like the Magi's gift of frankincense: burn candles, light incense, and display potpourri to create fragrant memories of God's presence.

Savor [Taste]

Scripture: Psalm 34:8

O taste and see that the Lord is good; happy are those who take refuge in him.

Advent

During Advent preparations, offer to another the tastes from your own kitchen, or from your favorite bakery, and enjoy the sense of growth that comes from sharing.

Christmas

Invite someone who otherwise might be alone to share the tastes of your Christmas table.

Epiphany

Experiment with recipes for dishes from other cultures and celebrate Christ's birth for all the world.

Feel [Touch]

Scripture: Matthew 9:21

For she said to herself, "If I only touch his cloak, I will be made well."

Advent

Offer to massage the shoulders of someone weary with the Christmas rush and welcome an exchange in kind!

Christmas

Hold hands with loved ones as you share Christmas memories.

Epiphany

Exchange handmade gifts from third world countries and bless the hands who crafted each one.

Look [Sight]

Scripture: Luke 2:30

For my eyes have seen your salvation.

Advent

Prepare to see the meaning of Christmas more clearly this year by doing some devotional reading each day of Advent.

Christmas

Visit churches to view their manger scenes and to appreciate the lights and displays of the season.

Epiphany

Go out each evening to view the stars, remembering the star that guided the magi to find Jesus, and ask God to guide your seeking.

Family Advent Festival

Celebrate Advent, and prepare for Christmas, as an individual family, with other households, or during an intergenerational gathering by holding a "Critters around the Crèche" Festival. Use the unique design—Gather! Explore! Celebrate! Share!—to get ready to experience Jesus' birth. The event may need to take place in two stages—one to mold the animal shapes since they need to dry overnight or longer and the other to decorate the figures and complete the wreath.

Gather

Gather the participants for music and an explanation of the program. Sing Advent hymns and Christmas carols that mention the animals in the scripture story or share the songs through recordings of the music.

Explore

Continue the event in a space where there are tables and chairs to construct the animal-themed Advent wreaths.

Materials

- Boxes, plates, or trays
- Candles—3 blue or purple, 1 pink, and 1 white
- Cookie cutter shapes or patterns for animals: camel, cow, dog, donkey, dove, and lamb
- Cotton, fake fur, trims, and yarn
- Holders for candles on wreath—4
- Holder for Christ candle
- Markers, permanent—various colors
- Model Magic™
- Pins, long
- Pipe cleaners, long
- Ribbon
- Rolling pins
- Scissors
- Wreaths—straw

Advance Preparation

Form the animal shapes from the Model Magic™ material as they must air-dry overnight. Model Magic is a Crayola product available in craft and hobby stores.

Method

Working as family units, construct Advent wreaths to use at home in conjunction with the theme "Critters around the Crèche."

Create the six animals needed for the wreath from a material called Model Magic™. Model Magic is a moldable, clay-like substance with a spongy, light texture. After it air-dries, it is no longer moldable but it still retains some of its sponginess. It is neither greasy nor smelly and it doesn't need to be baked. To make the animals, form pieces of Model Magic into balls, flatten with the hand, and roll the material until it is approximately ⅛ to ¼ inches thick. If possible, use cookie cutter animal forms to cut out the shape of the camel, cow, dog, donkey, dove, and lamb. If cookie cutters are not available, trace animal patterns onto the dough and cut out the shapes with a craft knife. If several families are involved in the event, place each set of completed animals in a separate box or on an individual plate or tray which has the name of the family printed on it. Allow the pieces to air-dry overnight or longer.

To decorate the animals, provide permanent markers in a variety of colors as well as craft materials such as cotton, fake fur, and yarn. Encourage creativity as each family enhances the six animals in their set.

For each project, use a straw wreath as the base. Decorate the wreath by winding ribbon around the circle. Pin the ribbon in place at appropriate places.

To attach the animal pieces to the top of the wreath, evenly space the figures around the circle. Strap one or two long pipe cleaners around each shape and tie them at the bottom. Trim off the excess pipe cleaner.

Space four individual plastic candle holders, used in floral arrangements, around the circumference of the wreath. Supply four purple candles, one to be lit each week of Advent. Also offer each family one white candle to be placed in a separate holder and set in the center of the wreath to light on Christmas Eve or Christmas Day.

Celebrate!

At the end of the activity, gather as a group and celebrate by singing a song, reading a scripture passage, and offering a prayer.

Share!

Begin to use the wreath on the First Sunday of Advent, continue for the remaining three weeks of the season, on Christmas Eve or Christmas Day, and re-light the Christ candle on Epiphany.

Sharing the Story

Christmas Pageant

"The Menagerie at the Manger"

Overview

As a companion to *Critters around the Crèche*, the resource *The Menagerie at the Manger* offers a complete guide for planning, preparing, and presenting a Christmas pageant based on the theme of the animals and the senses. Share the stories explored and experienced in church, home, and school settings during the season of Advent with a broader audience of parishioners in the congregation; family members in immediate and extended households; and classmates, parents, and teachers in educational settings by offering this joyful celebration of the Christmas story to members of the community.

The Menagerie at the Manger resource is organized into three sections to help churches and schools—as well as groups and families—prepare for a presentation of a unique Christmas program celebrating the birth of Jesus, our Savior.

The three segments are:

- Plan the Program
- Prepare the Parts
- Present the Pageant.

Plan the Program, the first section of the book, contains an overview of each component of the production. Beginning with a theme statement and a short summary, the Plan chapter contains an overview of cast, personnel, costumes, props, equipment, music, and setting. It includes a basic timetable to guide the process as well as suggestions for rehearsals. Charts listing themes and age groups as well as cast, costumes, equipment, and props provide at-a-glance checklists to guide preparation.

Prepare the Parts, segment two, details activities for each age/grade involved in *Menagerie*. Responsibilities for each group are organized into Activity, Before the Pageant, and During the Pageant sections. Instructions for preparation of costumes, props, and scenarios are detailed for each category of participants, too.

Present the Pageant, part three, provides a complete, detailed script as well as an outline for a bulletin/program for the celebration.

The Menagerie at the Manger is a minimal rehearsal pageant. Preparation for the five scenes, as well as the opening and closing segments, can be done in three class sessions. One full rehearsal prior to the presentation, or even before the event, is all that is necessary to offer a meaningful Christmas celebration for family and friends as well as for the participants themselves.

Themes At a Glance

Pageant	*Theme*	*Scripture*	*Sense*	*Animal*
Gather to Celebrate	Introduction/Preparation for Program	-	-	-
Tell the Story: Scene One	The Christmas Story Begins: Hear Love	Luke 2:1-5	Sound	Donkey
Tell the Story: Scene Two	All Is Now Ready: Smell Hope	Luke 2:6-7	Smell	Dog
Tell the Story: Scene Three	The Angel's Announcement: Taste Peace	Luke 2:8-14	Taste	Dove
Tell the Story: Scene Four	The Stable Is Crowded: Touch Joy	Luke 2:15-16	Touch	Cow
Tell the Story: Scene Five	The Baby Is Jesus: See Light	Luke 2:17-20	Sight	Lamb
Share the Message	Conclusion	John 1:1-5	-	-

All groups, Kindergarten through High School, sing in the choir and participate in the closing nativity scene. If younger children, such as nursery and preschool aged boys and girls are included in the program, they may sing in the choir and participate in the closing tableau as well.

Advent Activities

Sight: Seeing the Story

Artists throughout history have illustrated the story of the coming of the Savior through a variety of methods and materials. The Annunciation, Nativity, Madonna and Child, Holy Family, Adoration of the Shepherds, Visit of the Magi, and Presentation in the Temple are among the themes.

During Advent, Christmas, and Epiphany observe several ways in which the stories have been depicted. Twenty-five painters, representing different periods of art, are listed together with the titles of their works. In addition, many places and ways to discover these seasonal scenes—in expected locations and unexpected settings—are suggested.

This activity can be done by one person, a team such as an immediate or extended family, a church or school class, or an intergenerational group. Those participating could meet in person and go to a variety of places, including churches, gift shops, and museums, to find the Christmas story depicted on works of art. The exercise may also be done online with teams searching for different types of items and on various sites. Once the research is concluded, or after a certain amount of time, the results can be shared by sending and posting pictures, meeting via video chat, or doing a show and tell using an online program. Regardless of who participates, how the information is gathered, and the method by which it is shared, the goal is to see the story in many and varied ways.

Painters and Paintings

- Angelico, Fra—*Madonna of Humility*
- Botticelli—*The Virgin Adoring the Child*
- Campin, Robert—*The Annunciation*
- Correggio—*The Annunciation*
- Crivelli, C.—*Madonna*
- Da Panicale, Masolino—*Annunciation*
- David, G.—*Virgin and Child*
- Da Vinci, Leonardo—*The Annunciation*
- DeFlandes, Juan—*The Annunciation*
- Del Sarto—*Holy Family*
- DiPaolo, G.—*The Annunciation*
- Duccio—*Nativity with the Prophets Isaiah and Ezekiel*
- Griogione—*Adoration of the Shepherds*
- El Greco—*Nativity*
- Grunewald, M.—*Nativity*
- Lippi, Fra Filippo—*The Annunciation*
- Lotto, Lorenzo—*The Nativity*
- Masters of the Barberini Panels—*The Annunciation*
- Memling, Hans—*The Presentation*
- Michelangelo—*Holy Family*
- Pierodi, Cosimo—*Nativity with the Infant St. John*
- Raphael—*The 'Coloma Madonna'*
- Tanner, Henry Ossawa—*The Annunciation*
- Titian—*The Madonna and Child*
- Van Eyck, Jan—*The Annunciation*

Suggestions for Seeing the Story

Appreciate the art on:

- Collectible plates
- Commemorative dishes

Branch out from painting and search for nativity scenes in other art media:

- Architecture
- Banners
- Mosaics
- Photographs
- Prints
- Sculpture
- Stained glass
- Tapestries
- Vestments.

Check out pictures in a classic, specialized coloring book like:

- Sibbett, Ed., Jr. *Cathedral Stained Glass Coloring Book*. New York: Dover Publications, 1980.

Discover drawings in prayer books.

Download a lecture from YouTube such as the National Gallery of Art's annual tour of their Christmas collection.

Examine pictures in Bibles.

Find illustrations in Bible story books.

Go to a library and page through art books.

Locate information in online or physical encyclopedias.

Notice the art on:

- Christmas cards
- Note cards and stationery
- Postcards
- Posters
- Postage stamps.

Page through books on periods of art such as Middle Ages, Renaissance, Spanish, and French.

Read biographies of artists.

Search websites that feature art with images of the nativity.

Take a virtual tour of a world-class museum that has many nativity-related pieces in their collection.

Tour a church and discover its Advent, Christmas, and Epiphany art in many places.

Visit an art museum and view the collection of paintings.

Watch a film about painting and painters.

Smell: Savor the Seasons

Smell, one of the five senses that humans use to discern their world, is the ability to perceive an odor or scent through the nose and the brain by means of the olfactory nerves. Studies indicate that smell is the sense that has the strongest impact on recall memory. During Advent, Christmas, and Epiphany the sense of smell plays a huge part in getting ready for, as well as enjoying, these seasons.

As a class, a family, or a group, explore the sense of smell as a way to make memories and to re-live them. Suggestions for four weeks of savoring the seasons during Advent are offered. They include:

Week One—Guess the Scent

Fill bags with edible items that have easy to identify smells, guess one each day, and enjoy the contents!

Week Two—Prepare the Scent

Make sniff-a-scent bottles to use as a guessing game every day for a week.

Week Three—Find the Scent

Become aware of smells in places in the community and share the findings with others.

Week Four—Share the Scent

Bake or cook a different holiday dish each day and savor the smells in the process. Enjoy, give away, or invite others to share the results.

Ideas for the twelve days of Christmas, as well as for Epiphany, might be:

Christmas and Epiphany—Give the Scent

Of course, many other ideas and items may be substituted during any of the days and weeks to make the project more personal.

Week One—Guess the Scent

Materials

- Bags, small brown paper or decorated holiday gift type—7
- Items for bags such as:
  - Candy cane or peppermint
  - Chocolate
  - Cinnamon stick
  - Evergreen branch, fresh
  - Gingerbread cake or cookies
  - Orange
  - Popcorn

Method

Fill each of seven brown paper lunch sacks or small holiday gift bags with one strong-smelling item that has a connection with the season. Share one bag a day for a week with the participants. Invite the group to sniff the item and make a guess to name it. If the object is edible, enjoy it!

Week Two—Prepare the Scent

Materials

- Bottles, small from spices or travel size containers
- Cotton balls—7 or more

- Envelopes, small brown (optional)
- Extracts, oils, or spices for scents such as:
- Almond
- Cinnamon
- Cloves
- Lemon
- Orange
- Peppermint
- Vanilla

Method

Make sensory smell bottles, or envelopes, to use as a guessing game with a group every day for a week. This would also be a great project to give as a gift to a family with children.

On each of seven cotton balls, put a few drops of an extract or oil such as almond or peppermint or rub it with a spice like cinnamon or cloves. Place each ball in a separate container. Offer one bottle per day, remove the lid if necessary, and invite the players to identify the smell.

Week Three—Find the Scent

Materials

- Notebook, paper, or phone
- Pen

Method

Be aware of aromas in the air while visiting places in the community. Locations, as well as possible scents, include:

- Bakery, Candy Store—Bread, Fudge
- Church—Candles, Incense
- Department Store—Fragrances
- Florist—Flowers
- Outside—Snow
- Restaurant—Food
- Zoo—Animals

Week Four—Share the Scent

Materials

- Equipment and supplies for selected recipes
- Ingredients for recipes

Method

Bake or cook a variety of holiday foods, one a day for a week, and savor the smells during the process. Give away the finished products or invite others to come to share the results.

Foods might include:

- Beverages—eggnog, hot chocolate, wassail
- Candy—divinity, fudge, Torrone (Italian candy)
- Cookies—rosettes, spritz, sugar
- Desserts—Buche de Noel (French log cake), fruitcake, plum pudding
- Meals—ham, lamb, turkey
- Pies—mince, pecan, pumpkin
- Side dishes—cranberries, green bean casserole, sweet potatoes.

Christmas and Epiphany—Give a Scent

Materials

Varied with gift

Method

During the twelve days of Christmas and on Epiphany, offer a small gift to someone each day. These could be actual items or they could be smells others can enjoy.

Thirteen items to give could be:

- After shave or perfume
- Air freshener for car
- Aromatherapy oils
- Bubble bath
- Coffee
- Flowers
- Fruit
- Grooming supplies
- Incense
- Lip balm
- Lotion
- Soap
- Tea

Ways to share smells might include:

- Bake a batch of cinnamon bread, cookies, or rolls
- Fry a pan of bacon
- Hang a sage wreath
- Light a scented candle
- Make a pot of flavored coffee or hot chocolate
- Place an air freshener in a cabinet
- Prepare scented fire starters
- Put sachets in drawers
- Refresh the evergreen branches on a centerpiece
- Set out a bowl of potpourri
- Spray a scent like evergreen
- Start a simmer pot
- Steep a pot of tea.

Regardless of the project picked and the experiences enjoyed, savor the seasons of Advent, Christmas, and Epiphany through the amazing sense of smell.

Service Projects

Sound: Advent Offering Calendar

During November and December, listen attentively to the variety of sounds that are heard during the holidays. Sounds may range from the crunch of straw in a stable to the music of a crowd of carolers. Look through the Bible and recall some of the noises associated with the scripture stories. Write a list of 25 sounds—refer to the suggestions provided—and use the ideas to create a unique Advent calendar. Record the list on a piece of paper, as a memo in a phone, on individuals strips for a paper chain, or on blank squares of a calendar page.

To use the project as an Advent calendar—as a class, a congregation, or a family—listen for a specific sound each day. Remember its significance to the season, but take the activity one step further by using the calendar as an outreach project. In advance, decide on a recipient of an offering and an amount of money—one cent, five cents, or more—to place in a bank each time the sound of the day is heard or made.

Suggested Sounds

Saw

Remember Joseph's profession as a carpenter.

Clip Clop

Recreate the sound of the donkey that carried Mary to Bethlehem or visit a live nativity scene and listen to the sound a donkey makes when walking.

Voices

Harken to the sounds of crowds and remember the travelers in the town of Bethlehem.

Coins

Simulate the sounds of the coins being dropped into Caesar's coffers.

Knock

Give an offering each time someone knocks on the door and recall the knock on the door of the inn.

No

Pretend each "no" heard today is the innkeeper saying "no room" to Mary and Joseph.

Straw

Recall the crunch of the straw in the stable.

Baa

Visit the zoo and listen to the noise of the sheep.

Moo

Go to a farm and hear the sounds of cows.

Silence

Reflect on the stillness of the night on which the Savior was born.

Cry

Relive the cry of the newborn infant by placing coins in the bank each time crying is heard.

Scripture

Read Luke 2 which records the birth of Jesus.

Bells

Capture the sound of church bells proclaiming the good news.

Carolers

Sing a carol or listen to a group of carolers.

Gloria

Repeat the words of the angels.

Peace on Earth

Rejoice at the message of the coming of the Messiah.

Wind

Whistle the sound that was heard in the field.

Feet

Recall the shepherds traveling to Bethlehem to worship the Babe.

Poem

Recite a poem which expresses emotions stirred by the event.

Crinkle of paper

Suggest the sound of unwrapping a gift.

Radio

Record a portion of a program with a Christmas theme.

Doorbell

Give a coin each time the doorbell rings as a reminder of guests and gifts that may arrive.

Bell Ringers

Renew a commitment to help those in need.

Laughter

Listen to the happy expressions of children who await Christmas.

Stores

Search for sounds of the true meaning of Christmas above the noises of the commercial emphasis.

Taste: Christmas Is for the Birds: Edible Gifts for God's Creatures

Christmas is for the birds. And, for that matter, so is every other day of the year. During the winter months—especially in areas of severe cold and heavy snow—God's people have the responsibility of caring for God's creatures. The seasons of Advent, Christmas and Epiphany offer many possibilities for designing projects that provide food for these winged wonders. Involve family and friends, as well as classes and congregations, in a variety of activities to make and give edible gifts to the birds. Select several of the following suggestions, provide the supplies, and guide the process. As a group, hang the completed projects in trees on the church or school property, or invite each person to take his or her creations home to share with feathered friends in the neighborhood. Remind the participants that once they start to feed the birds, they will keep coming back for more. In fact, the birds will start to depend on these treats for their sustenance. Challenge people to make the commitment to continue the feeding process throughout the winter. Gift-givers might also leave a dish of fresh water somewhere near the feeder for the visitors to enjoy.

Bacon Balls

Materials

- Bacon grease
- Bags, nylon mesh
- Birdseed
- Cornmeal
- Mixing bowl and utensils
- Sand
- Scissors
- String

Method

To make bacon balls, add birdseed and cornmeal to room temperature bacon grease. Mix until it is a doughy consistency. Add sand, if desired, for grit. Put portions of the mixture into separate mesh bags and tie them shut. Hang each bacon ball in a tree. The birds will perch on the netting as they enjoy the treat.

Bird Pudding

Materials

- Bacon grease
- Bread crumbs
- Cups, paper or plastic
- Mixing bowl and utensils
- Oatmeal, cooked
- Potatoes, leftover

- Raisins
- Scissors
- String

Method

Combine bread crumbs, extra cooked potatoes, leftover cooked oatmeal, and raisins. Place the mixture in paper or plastic cups. Pour a little bacon grease over the concoction and let it harden. Poke a hole in each cup, make a loop of string through the opening, and hang each cup on a branch so visiting birds can enjoy this pudding.

Birdseed Cookies

Materials

- Birdseed
- Bread
- Cookie cutters
- Cornmeal
- Knives
- Mixing bowl and utensils
- Nails
- Peanut butter
- Scissors
- Yarn

Method

In advance, lay out the bread so it becomes hard and stale. Make a mixture of one part cornmeal and three parts peanut butter. When the participants arrive, cut a slice of bread with a cookie cutter. Make a hole in the top of the bread with a nail. Thread a length of yarn approximately one-foot long through the hole and tie the ends together. Spread the top of the bread cookie with the peanut butter mixture. Sprinkle with birdseed. Continue the process until the ingredients are depleted. Hang the cookies in a tree for the birds to enjoy.

Birdseed Pretzels

Materials

- Birdseed
- Peanut butter
- Pretzel sticks or twists
- Scissors
- String or yarn

Method

For birdseed pretzels, tie a loop of string or yarn through the top of a large pretzel stick or a pretzel twist. Cover the pretzel with peanut butter and roll it in birdseed. Hang it on the limb of a tree.

Bird Treats

Materials

- Aluminum foil pieces or paper muffin cups
- Bags, mesh (optional)
- Bird seed
- Meat drippings (optional)
- Muffin tins
- Nuts, chopped
- Pan, heavy weight
- Raisins, chopped
- Suet
- Sunflower seeds
- Wire (optional)

Method

Line muffin tins with aluminum foil pieces or paper muffin cups. Set aside. Melt the suet in a heavy saucepan. Stir in broken nuts, chopped raisins, and various seeds. Ladle the mixture into the tins and set them in the refrigerator overnight. When hardened, remove the cakes from the tins. Serve them to the birds in mesh bags or place them in tree cavities. They can also be wired to the side of a feeder or crumbled into an open pie tin. Leftover cakes may be stored in the freezer.

Coffee Can Feeders

Materials

- Aluminum pie tins
- Birdseed
- Bottle opener
- Coffee cans
- Rope or string
- Sunflower seeds
- Wire
- Wire cutter

Method

Construct bird feeders from coffee cans and pie tins. For each feeder, use a bottle opener to punch several holes around the bottom of a coffee can. Poke holes at the top of the can and make a loop of rope, string, or wire to use as the hanger. Fill the can with birdseed or sunflower seeds. Place an aluminum pie tin over the open end, poke holes through the can and the plate, and connect the two pieces with wire. Turn over the feeder and hang it on the branch of a tree.

Corn Feeders

Materials

- Corn, dry ears
- Hangers, wire

Method

Use a wire hanger to make a hook for hanging each ear of dried corn. Be sure to push the ends of the wire into the corn ear so the birds won't hurt themselves while feasting. Attach the corn to a tree.

Doughnut Decorations

Materials

- Doughnuts, stale
- Floral wire or string
- Scissors

Method

Tie stale doughnuts to a tree branch with floral wire or string.

Fruit Baskets

Materials

- Birdseed
- Bread cubes
- Grapefruit or orange halves
- Pipe cleaners
- Suet chunks

Method

To create fruit baskets, fill empty grapefruit or orange halves with a combination of bread cubes, mixed seeds, and suet chunks. Attach pipe cleaners at three places around the edge of the fruit; join them at the center and twist to form a hook to use to hang the feeders on branches.

Fruit Kebabs

Materials

- Bread products
- Cord, heavy, or metal or wooden skewers
- Fruit pieces such as apples, cranberries, dates, oranges
- Peanuts, unshelled
- Scissors
- String

Method

On a heavy cord or a metal or wooden skewer, string a combination of apple slices, bread cubes, cranberries, dates, orange sections, stale doughnuts, suet, and unshelled peanuts. Tie a loop of string around the top and hang each kebab in a tree.

Grain Goodies

Materials

- Grain sheaves such as barley, oat, wheat
- Pine cones
- Ribbon

Method

Tie ribbon around several pieces of barley, oats, and wheat. Add a few pine cones, if desired. Hang each goodie on a tree branch.

Gourd Feeders

Materials

- Birdseed
- Gourds
- Hammer
- Knife
- Nails

Method

Gourds, of all shapes and sizes, make interesting bird feeders. Select gourds with hard skin and a dry stem. Hammer two nail holes near the stem. Cut a wide circle out of one side, empty out the seeds, loop a string through the holes, and hang up the bird feeder. Fill the feeder with birdseed or other items the flying friends will enjoy.

Milk Carton Feeders

Materials

- Aluminum pie plates
- Bottles, plastic, from bleach or detergent and cartons from milk—empty and thoroughly washed
- Glue
- Hangers, wire with cardboard tubes
- Scissors
- Tape

Method

Use a large milk carton or an empty plastic bottle for each feeder. Cut a large hole in the side for a door. Leave the door attached at the top to use as a flap to keep out the rain. Attach an aluminum pie plate to the bottom with glue or tape and another to the top to make a roof. Stick the cardboard tube from the hanger through for a perch and use the wire portion for hanging up the feeder. Fill the feeder with seeds or other tidbits and wait for the birds to find it.

Peanut Projects

Materials

- Peanuts in the shell
- Scissors
- String or thread

Method

Tie peanuts along a piece of heavy string or thread and tie it to a tree branch.

Pine Cone Feeders

Materials

- Knives
- Peanut butter
- Pine cones

- Scissors
- String

Method

Select a pine cone and tie a six inch piece of yarn around the base of it. Then loop and tie the yarn in a bow for easy hanging. Use a knife to spread peanut butter on the layers of the pine cone. Roll it in birdseed. Hang the feeder on a branch.

Popcorn Strings

Materials

- Cranberries
- Floral wire
- Popcorn, popped
- Raisins

Method

String popcorn, as well as cranberries and raisins on pieces of floral wire. Bend the wire and attach the ends to form a circle that can be hung over branches.

Snow Person Projects

Materials

- Birdseed
- Bread sticks
- Cranberries
- Fruit, dried varieties such as apricots, dates, prunes, and raisins
- Peanut butter
- Pine cones
- Popcorn, popped
- Snow
- String
- Suet
- Twigs

Method

Construct a large snow person. Use strong twigs for the arms. Create the nose from a bread stick or a pine cone covered with peanut butter and birdseed or with suet. Use prunes for the eyes and dates and raisins for the mouth. Try dried apricots for buttons. String cranberries and popcorn and add the garland as a belt around the middle and a band around a hat.

Touch: Gifts That Touch Others

At Christmas, God gave his Son, Jesus, to be the Savior of the world. In response to this great gift, people continue to give and receive presents as signs of love for God and for others. This activity involves gifts which cost little or no money, Give them to family, friends, neighbors, and others as expressions of gratitude to God.

Materials

- Bow
- Markers
- Paper, Christmas gift wrap
- Paper, construction
- Shoe box
- Tape, cellophane

Method

Prepare a box to hold the 25 "Touch" gift suggestions. Cover the lid and the bottom of a shoe box with Christmas paper. Wrap the two pieces separately. Tape a bow on the cover. Cut twenty-five strips of construction paper and write one "gift" on each piece. Choose from the suggestions provided, or brainstorm additional ideas. Place the strips in the box and put the cover on it. Choose a strip and give a "Touching Gift" each day for twenty-five days.

Gift Suggestions

- Babysit for someone with a small child.
- Bake bread and give a loaf away.
- Become a pen pal with someone in another country.
- Bring a small decorated tree to someone who doesn't have one.
- Call neighborhood children to come play games.
- Craft favors to be used on hospital trays.
- Create Christmas ornaments that can be given away.
- Deliver food baskets to those in need.
- Eat simply and give the saved money to a charity.
- Go caroling in the neighborhood.
- Have a family cleaning day and cooperate to prepare for the Christmas "Guest."
- Help prepare a family meal.
- Invite a friend for cocoa and conversation.
- Make cookies and give a dozen away.
- Offer a smile and a friendly word to a sales clerk.
- Pray for each member of the family.
- Prepare Christmas cards for shut-ins.
- Read the Christmas story to someone with poor sight.
- Share gently used toys with community agencies.
- Shovel or sweep the sidewalk of a neighbor.
- Take a person who doesn't drive shopping.
- Visit a long-lived person.
- Volunteer in a soup kitchen.
- Write a letter to a loved one.

References

Companion Resources

Critters around the Crèche is one of three resources in a set that can be used together, or individually, to connect the five senses with the liturgical year. The two additional tools, also published by The Pastoral Center, are detailed here.

The Menagerie at the Manger: Children's Christmas Pageant

Phyllis Vos Wezeman and Anna L. Liechty
Alameda, CA: The Pastoral Center, 2021

This guidebook seeks to make the Christmas story come alive by imagining what animals might have been present at the time of Jesus' birth. Using this broad theme, each animal brings a unique physical sense to the story at the stable—hearing, seeing, smelling, tasting, touching—which helps humans learn an Advent message: how to wait in hope, joy, love, and peace in order to live in God's light.

It is organized into three sections:

- **Plan the Program** contains an overview of each component of the production. It includes a basic timetable to guide the process as well as suggestions for rehearsals. Charts provide "At-a-Glance" checklists to guide preparation.
- **Prepare the Parts** details activities for each age/grade, organized into Activity, Before the Pageant, and During the Pageant. Includes guidelines for music and reproducible outlines for animals used in the program.
- **Present the Pageant** provides a complete, detailed script as well as an outline for a bulletin/program for the celebration. Charts in this section offer an "At-a-Glance" reference for each scene.

8½"x11" • 66 PAGES

DOWNLOADABLE & REPRODUCIBLE

DOWNLOADABLE REPRODUCIBLE SHARABLE AFFORDABLE

Sensing the Seasons: 40 Learning Centers for the Church Year

Phyllis Vos Wezeman and Anna L. Liechty
Alameda, CA: The Pastoral Center, 2020

What does Advent taste like? What does Christmas feel like? What does Ordinary Time smell like? What does Lent sound like? What does Easter look like?

This collection of 40 activities will help people of all ages explore and experience seven significant periods of the liturgical cycle. Each chapter features a period, offering one learning center activity for each of the five senses. Use them in the classroom, for family or intergenerational events, in worship settings such as Children's Liturgy of the Word, or at any other time when you can invite believers to enter the church year experientially.

These creative activities will remind learners to get ready for the Messiah during Advent, celebrate the birth of the Savior at Christmas, rejoice in God's gift of the Christ Child throughout Epiphany, remember the life and ministry of Jesus in Lent, commemorate the Savior's death and resurrection at Easter, share the Good News of God's love during Pentecost, and grow as disciples throughout Ordinary Time.

8½"x11" • 120 PAGES

DOWNLOADABLE WITH OPTIONAL PAPERBACK

- Sensing the Church Year
  - Clock Face Calendars (Sight)
  - Colorful Weavings (Smell)
  - Bottle Scale Songs (Sound)
  - Snack Sacks (Taste)
  - Beaded Pins (Touch)
- Sensing Advent
  - Decorated Candles (Sight)
  - Lavender Sachets (Smell)
  - Music Mobiles (Sound)
  - Cookie Gifts (Taste)
  - Mini Wreaths (Touch)
- Sensing Christmas
  - Stained Glass Ornaments (Sight)
  - Pomander Balls (Smell)
  - Mini Jingle Bell Wreaths (Sound)
  - Gingerbread with Toppings (Taste)
  - Evergreen Prints (Touch)
- Sensing Epiphany
  - Sand Painted Cards (Sight)
  - Incense Holders (Smell)
  - Sound Effects (Sound)
  - Crisp Rice Star Treats (Taste)
  - Shell Covered Chests (Touch)
- Sensing Lent
  - Cross Symbols (Sight)
  - Scented Soap Balls (Smell)
  - Prayer Poems (Sound)
  - Lenten Foods Concentration Game (Taste)
  - Educational Eggs (Touch)
- Sensing Easter
  - Butterfly Banners (Sight)
  - Egg Decorations (Smell)
  - Flower Pot Bells (Sound)
  - Butterfly Shaped Snacks (Taste)
  - Block Print Cards (Touch)
- Sensing Pentecost
  - Trinity Triptych (Sight)
  - Guided Meditation (Smell)
  - Bottle Puppets (Sound)
  - Meringues (Taste)
  - Dove Mobiles (Touch)
- Sensing Ordinary Time
  - Wire Fish Pendants (Sight)
  - Herb Bottles and Gardens (Smell)
  - Rhythm Instruments (Sound)
  - Memorizing Bible Verses (Taste)
  - Flowering Branches (Touch)

About the Authors

Anna L. Liechty

Anna Liechty taught English to high school students and served as adjunct faculty for Indiana University. Anna also worked as a mentor trainer and teacher coach with adult learners for the Indiana Department of Education. She won numerous educational classroom grants, including the Eli Lilly Teacher Creativity grant.

As a life-long church educator, Anna worked with all age levels, directing Sunday morning and youth programming, consulting with congregations about their educational ministry, and writing a wide variety of religious education materials. She served as Vice President of Active Learning Associates and co-authored four Lilly Worship Renewal grants.

Anna's undergraduate degree is from Bowling Green State University in Ohio and her Master's degree from Indiana University South Bend. She was certified by the National Board for Professional Teaching Standards in Adolescent and Young Adult English Language Arts.

In retirement, Anna continues to pursue a variety of writing projects, receiving an Individual Artist Grant in Literature from the Indiana Arts Commission. Now living in Florida, Anna enjoys traveling with her husband Page Foster, a retired pastor, and counting the days between visits with six children, twelve grandchildren, and seven great-grandchildren.

Phyllis Vos Wezeman

As a religious educator, Phyllis Wezeman has served as Director of Christian Nurture at a downtown congregation in South Bend, Indiana; Executive Director of the Parish Resource Center of Michiana; and Program Coordinator for ecumenical as well as interfaith organizations in Indiana and Michigan.

In academics, Phyllis has been Adjunct Faculty in the Education Department at Indiana University South Bend and in the Department of Theology at the University of Notre Dame. She is an "Honorary Professor" of the Saint Petersburg (Russia) State University of Pedagogical Art where she has taught methods courses for extended periods on several occasions. She has also been guest lecturer at the Shanghai Teachers College in China.

As founder of the not-for-profit Malawi Matters, Inc., she develops and directs HIV & AIDS Education programs with thousands of volunteers in 200 villages and more than 1,500 schools in Malawi, Africa including "Creative Methods of HIV & AIDS Education," "Culture & HIV-AIDS," and "Equipping Women/ Empowering Girls."

Author or co-author of over 2,000 articles and books, she has written for over 80 publishers.

Phyllis served as President of Active Learning Associates, Inc.; a consultant or board member to numerous local and national organizations such as the American Bible Society, Church World Service, LOGOS, and the Peace Child Foundation; leader of a six-week youth exchange program to Russia and Ukraine; and Project Director for four Lilley Worship Renewal grants. She is the recipient of three "Distinguished Alumni Awards," the Aggiornamento Award from the Catholic Library Association, and the 2021 Lifetime Achievement Award from the Association of Presbyterian Church Educators (APCE).

Wezeman holds undergraduate degrees in Business, Communications, and General Studies from various institutions and an MS in Education from Indiana University South Bend.

Phyllis and her husband Ken (who met when they were in second and third grade in elementary school) have three children and their spouses, Stephanie (Jeff), David, and Paul (Deha); five grandchildren, Quin, Ayle, Lief, Ashley, and Jacob; and two great-grandsons, Maddox and Troy.

by Anna L. Liechty & Phyllis Vos Wezeman

Experience the Saints • 4 Volumes

Activities for Multiple Intelligences

Eight activities per saint, each based on a different learning intelligence. Includes whole family and general classroom guides, with reproducible handouts.

- Vol. 1: Patrick, James, Hildegard of Bingen
- Vol. 2: Francis, Clare, Margaret of Scotland
- Vol. 3: Joan of Arc, Thomas Becket, Agnes
- Vol. 4: Peter, Catherine of Siena, Scholastica

200 PAGES PER VOLUME • 8½"x11" • DOWNLOADABLE

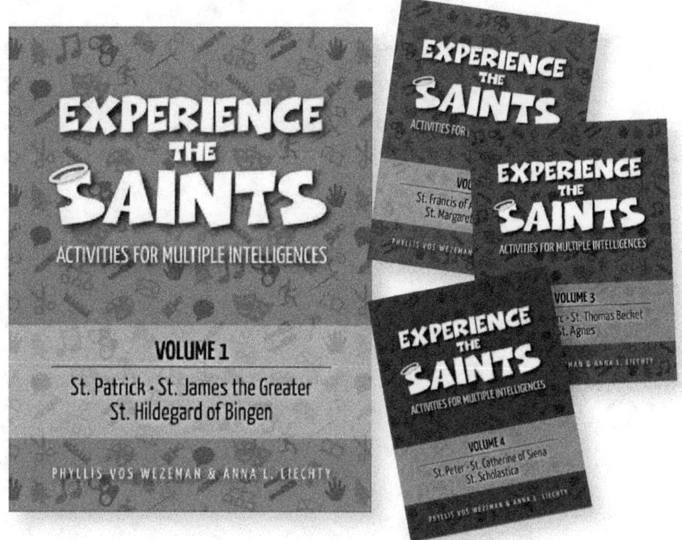

Seasons by Step: A Week-by-Week Thematic Approach

Use these creative approaches to explore a theme in-depth over the course of a season through Scripture. Each includes **talking points for children's messages, at-home family activities, artwork** for weekly symbols, and more.

Know Chocolate for Lent *(Lent & Holy Week)*

Uses the growing and manufacturing process of chocolate as a metaphor for the growth of faith and discipleship in the Christian life. Tools for parish-wide approach sold separately.

80 PAGES • DOWNLOADABLE

God's Family Tree *(Lent & Holy Week)*

Tracing the Story of Salvation

Tells the story of God's people as they struggle to find faith and hope for life through the symbols of trees found in Scripture. Includes optional Easter pageant and classroom activities.

114 PAGES • DOWNLOADABLE

In the Name of the Master *(Advent/Christmas/Epiphany)*

Sharing the Story of Christ

Uses a variation of the Advent wreath that uses fruits as symbols for the many names of God's Masterpiece, Jesus. Help your kids & families go deeper as they light their Advent candles each week.

37 PAGES • DOWNLOADABLE

http://pastoral.center/phyllis-vos-wezeman

Pastoral ministers serving pastoral ministers

http://pastoral.center • resources@pastoralcenter.com • Call us at 844-727-8672 (M-F 9am-5pm CT)

www.ingramcontent.com/pod-product-compliance
Lightning Source LLC
LaVergne TN
LVHW080320110826
845155LV00026B/172

* 9 7 8 1 9 4 9 6 2 8 2 7 2 *